SUNSHINE

by the same author

THE BEACH
THE TESSERACT
28 DAYS LATER
THE COMA

SUNSHINE

ALEX GARLAND

ff
faber and faber

Faber and Faber, Inc.
An affiliate of Farrar, Straus and Giroux
18 West 18th Street, New York 10011

Printed in the United States of America
Originally published in 2007 by Faber and Faber Limited, Great Britain
Published in the United States by Faber and Faber, Inc.
First American edition, 2007

Library of Congress Cataloging-in-Publication Data
Garland, Alex, 1970–
Sunshine / Alex Garland.
p. cm.
ISBN-13: 978-0-571-23397-7

I. Title.

PN1997.2.S86 2002
822'.914—dc22
2007300350

www.fsgbooks.com

P1

Contents

Introduction

ALEX GARLAND

Sunshine was created out of a love of science, and of science fiction. In the same way that *28 Days Later* attempted to look back towards older post-apocalyptic stories, such as *Dawn of the Dead* and *Day of the Triffids*, *Sunshine* looked back to films such as *2001*, *Alien*, *Dark Star* and the original *Solaris*. This was slow-paced, outer-space science fiction. Hallucinatory sci fi about star travel and feeling claustrophobic while gazing into the void. A sub-genre, linked by a common theme: that what man finds in deep space is his unconscious.

Aside from being a love letter to its antecedents, I wrote *Sunshine* as a film about atheism. A crew is en route to a God-like entity: the Sun. The Sun is larger and more powerful than we can imagine. The Sun gave us life, and can take it away. It is nurturing, in that it provides the means of our survival, but also terrifying and hostile, in that it will blind us if we look directly upon it, and its surface is as lethal to man as an environment can get.

As the crew travel nearer to the Sun, the majesty of the burning star fries their minds. The crew are hypnotised by it, or baffled by it, or driven mad by it. Ultimately, even the most rational crew member is overwhelmed by his sense of wonder and, as he falls into the star, he believes he is touching the face of God.

But he isn't. The Sun is God-like, but not God. Not a conscious being. Not a divine architect. And the crew member is only doing what man has always done: making an awestruck category error when confronted with our small place within the vast and neutral scheme of things.

The director, Danny Boyle, who is not atheistic in the way that I am, felt differently. He believed that the crew actually *were* meeting God. I didn't see this as a major problem, because the difference in our approach wasn't in conflict with the way in which the story would be told. The two interpretations that could be made from the narrative were the same two interpretations that could be made from the world around us. In that respect, perhaps the difference was even appropriate.

Cast and Crew

Sunshine received its world premiere in London in April 2007

PRINCIPAL CAST
(*in order of appearance*)

SEARLE	Cliff Curtis
VOICE OF ICARUS	Chipo Chung
CAPA	Cillian Murphy
CORAZON	Michelle Yeoh
KANEDA	Hiroyuki Sanada
CASSIE	Rose Byrne
TREY	Benedict Wong
MACE	Chris Evans
HARVEY	Troy Garity
PINBACKER	Mark Strong
CAPA'S SISTER	Paloma Baeza
CHILDREN	Archie Macdonald
	Sylvie Macdonald

PRINCIPAL CREW

Directed by	Danny Boyle
Written by	Alex Garland
Produced by	Andrew Macdonald
Director of Photography	Alwin Küchler
Production Designer	Mark Tildesley
Film Editor	Chris Gill
Visual Effects Supervisor	Tom Wood
Co-Producer	Bernard Bellow
Music by	John Murphy and Underworld
Costume Designer	Suttirat Anne Larlarb
Casting by	Donna Isaacson and Gail Stevens

Sunshine is presented by Fox Searchlight Pictures and DNA Films
in association with the UK Film Council and Ingenious Film Partners
Sunshine is a DNA Films production

Sunshine

THE SCREENPLAY

Open on:

Black screen.

Total darkness, with a pinprick of light in the center.

PINBACKER
(*voice-over*)
Those stars are the fleshed forebears of these dark hills, bowed like labourers, and of my blood.

Silence.

The death of a gnat is a star's mouth: its skin, like Mary's or Semele's, thin as the skin of fire: a star fell on her. A sun devoured her.

Suddenly, cut from darkness to blinding light, and . . .

EXT. THE SURFACE OF THE SUN

It never coalesces. It's something we can't quite comprehend. Too much power, too massive, too ancient.

The image boils and rages, and is completely hypnotic.

The noise is overwhelming.

Over this, the title:

SUNSHINE

EXT. THE SUN

. . . The curve of the Sun against the dark of space, where solar flares arc thousands of miles, before the vast gravity of the star pulls them back . . .

EXT. SPACE

. . . Now tens of millions of miles distant from the star, where the sound of fission and countless rolling nuclear detonations are silent in the vacuum . . .

EXT. ICARUS II

. . . a spaceship is heading towards the Sun.

The ship is a slender living area, rotating to create a centrifuge gravitational effect. The living area is positioned behind a vast circular shield – gently curving, formed of innumerable mirrored gold panels.

In the shadow of the shield, we can see the form of multiple huge booster-rockets, and a large shape which we will later learn is the payload.

The distances involved are so huge between the ship and the Sun that it hardly seems to be moving.

But as we get closer, and we see space dust and particles flash past or colliding with the shield, detonating and burning under the impact and friction, we realize that in fact the ship is travelling at an extraordinarily fast speed.

On the spaceship's side is its name: ICARUS II.

INT. CORRIDOR

In the main corridor that runs through Icarus II two men sit on the floor, arms folded, their faces a picture of deep thought.

The first, and older, of these two men is Captain Akira Kaneda. The Icarus II is under his command. He's a career astronaut. Implacable, calm, experienced.

The younger of the two men is Capa. Capa is a career physicist. In contrast to Kaneda, Capa is thin, young, nervy, unkempt. He has a couple of weeks' beard growth, and his hair is bedraggled.

Between them is a chess board – sparse pieces, scattered. The end game.

Kaneda is playing white. Noticeably, the White King is made of silver.

Silence.

No movement from either of them.

The moment is held.

And held.

Finally, Kaneda puffs out his cheeks and expels a loud sigh. He reaches for his Silver King, and tips it over.

He has resigned.

Capa nods.

KANEDA

Good game.

They shake hands.

Capa checks his watch.

CAPA

Three and a half hours.

KANEDA

A long one.

CAPA

Really takes it out of you. All that concentration.

KANEDA

Yeah. It does.

A moment.

Then silently both men start to reset the board to play again.

INT. OXYGEN GARDEN

Corazon, a woman in her early thirties, a biologist, kneels beside a tall tree-fern, using secateurs to trim away dead fronds.

She is in the Oxygen Garden: a large room with a sloping roof, into which a glass corridor projects.

At the far end of the garden, where Corazon works, are a collection of ferns and dense green shrubs. There is also a pool, formed by condensation that runs down the sloping roof.

At the other end is a greenhouse, in which baby plants are nurtured.

Set into the sloping roof is a thick glass observation portal.

Most striking of all, however, are the high walls either side of the garden. Set into the walls are multiple drums – and inside each drum is a cylinder of grasses. The grasses grow evenly, three hundred and sixty degrees around the interior curve.

At the back of the drums are fans, rotating slowly, providing a breeze that gently ripples the grasses and gives them life.

INT. FLIGHT DECK

On the Flight Deck of the Icarus II, two more astronauts sit in front of their instrument panels, which glitters with back-lit displays and switches.

These are Cassie and Mace – flight crew, in the pilot and engineer's seats.

But neither have their seat straps on, or look like they are doing much in the way of piloting.

Mace, the engineer, has his seat reclined and is dozing, his chin on his chest and his feet propped up on the instrument panel.

Cassie, the pilot, is reading a book.

The book is Lady Chatterley's Lover.

Mace stirs in his sleep, and his foot shifts . . .

. . . flicking a switch to 'off' position with his heel.

Cassie, engrossed in her novel, hasn't noticed.

INT. ICARUS MAINFRAME

The ship's flight computer: four glass circuit panels, submerged in a tank of coolant.

The mainframe is housed in a room off the Flight Deck, behind a thick transparent divider. On the other side of the divider, we can see Cassie reading.

The circuitry on the panels is cosmically intricate, beautiful.

Beneath the surface of the liquid, lights flicker along the circuitry pathways. These flickers are synapse sparks of the flight computer's semi-consciousness.

Suddenly, the frequency and number of the lit pathways flare up.

As this happens, a digital temperature readout on the side of the tank moves up from minus 14.89 degrees Celsius to minus 13.13.

INT. FLIGHT DECK

ELECTRONIC VOICE

Warning. Coolant from port stabilizer redirected to rear engines. No extra coolant in rear engines required. Recommend coolant redirection is cancelled.

Cassie, unconcerned, not looking up from her book:

CASSIE

Fine.

The switch flicks itself back.

ELECTRONIC VOICE

Coolant redirection cancelled.

Cassie doesn't bother to respond . . .

. . . but does reach out with her hand to swipe at Mace's legs.

Grumbling through his sleep, Mace takes his feet off the instrument panel and rolls over onto his side.

INT. SLEEPING QUARTERS

The Comms Officer is asleep in his bunk, visible only as a silhouette behind the frosted-glass privacy partition.

We can't see him, but the name on his bunk reads: HARVEY.

Abruptly the lights come on. Followed by music, piped through his bunk's personal speakers.

ELECTRONIC VOICE

Harvey. Wake-up call.

Harvey sits up, blinking against the brightness, rubbing the sleep from his eyes.

HARVEY

Already?

He checks his watch.

Jesus.

INT. SOCIAL AREA

In the social area, the Navigation Officer, Trey is preparing food for the entire crew.

Above the small kitchenette surface we can see his name circled on the rota.

He hums to himself quietly as he prepares the food.

Trey is clearly an expert and rather obsessive chef, slicing paper-thin slivers of garlic.

Behind him, Corazon enters with vegetables from the Oxygen Garden.

INT. OBSERVATION ROOM

The Observation Room is three walls and a huge window. The room is at the most forward position of the Icarus II, therefore this window faces the Sun.

But the window is darkened greatly.

The Sun is only visible as a dull orange orb surrounded by blackness.

The room itself is only lit by the dull orange . . .

. . . but in the gloom, sitting on the observation couch, facing the window, we can see a man.

Searle – the doctor and psychiatrist of Icarus II.

SEARLE

Icarus.

The electronic voice, the voice of Icarus, replies:

ICARUS

Yes, Dr Searle.

SEARLE

Please re-filter the Observation Room portal.

ICARUS

Filter up or down, Dr Searle?

SEARLE

Up.

And the light levels dial up.

The room brightens considerably. We can see Searle clearly now. He is one of the older crew members – in his late thirties.

He gazes at the Sun, fascinated. Though still distant, the star is much larger and closer than we have ever seen it on Earth.

Searle is as hypnotized by the sight as we were during the opening sequence.

SEARLE

Icarus – how close is this to full brightness?

ICARUS

At this distance of thirty-six million miles, you are observing the sun at two percent of full brightness.

SEARLE

(*smiling*)

Two percent . . . Can you show me four percent?

ICARUS

Four percent would result in irreversible damage to your retinas. However, you could observe three point one percent, for a period of not longer than thirty seconds.

A moment. Then Searle taps some numbers into the filter console.

SEARLE

Icarus – I'm going to change the filter to three point one percent.

An amazing blast of bleaching brightness fills the room.

Searle sucks in a gasp, like a man diving into ice water.

Fade to white.

INT. SOCIAL AREA

The whiteness becomes the flash of stills cameras, taking photos of the entire crew.

The crew are all smiling, gazing directly at us.

And all wearing Christmas hats.

Freeze on one of these images – then pull back, to reveal that this is a framed crew photo, hanging in the social area of Icarus II.

The social area contains space to eat, relax and take briefings.

In the mess section, the entire crew of Icarus II are sitting down to eat.

Mace waits as his plate is elaborately prepared by Trey, and sprinkled lightly with fresh herbs.

Impatient, Mace sticks his finger in the sauce and takes a taste.

MACE

What is it – beef?

Trey bristles.

TREY

Chicken. (*Defensively.*) You don't like it, take my shift next time.

MACE

No, no. I love challenging cuisine.

Searle sits with Capa and Corazon.

SEARLE

Have you spent much time in the Observation Room recently?

CAPA

Some.

SEARLE

Has it ever occurred to you to dial up the filter?

Capa shakes his head.

SEARLE

Try it. It's invigorating. It's like taking a shower. In light. (*Beat.*) You lose yourself a little.

CORAZON

Like a flotation tank.

SEARLE

Actually, no. For psych-tests on deep space, I've run many sensory deprivation trials, testing total darkness in flotation tanks. The point about darkness is: you float in it. You and the darkness are distinct from each other because darkness is a vacuum, an *absence* of something, whereas we *are* something.

Searle pauses.

But total light envelopes you. It becomes you.

Searle laughs.

Anyway. It's very strange. I recommend it.

Mace is passing with his tray of food.

MACE

What's strange is, you're the psych officer on this ship, and I'm clearly a lot saner than you.

Now following Mace . . .

. . . who sits with Kaneda, Cassie and Harvey.

MACE

So – if no one else is going to mention it, I will.

KANEDA

The solar wind reading is much higher than we'd anticipated at this distance.

All look to Harvey – Comms Officer and Second-in-Command.

HARVEY

For the moment, we can still send package messages back. High frequency bursts will rise above the interference, and the Moon stations will pick them up. (*Beat.*) But it's possible that within twenty-four hours we won't be able to communicate at all.

KANEDA

Possible?

HARVEY

Probable.

Cassie gives a little shiver.

CASSIE

We'll finally be on our own.

Mace shrugs.

MACE

We're fifty-five million miles from Earth. We're already on our own.

All in the Mess Room have now fallen quiet. They listen to Kaneda speak.

KANEDA

We were expecting this. No great drama – we're flying into the dead zone seven days sooner than we thought. But if any of you were planning on sending a final message home, you should do it now.

INT. FLIGHT DECK/COMMS CUBICLE

Capa sits in a small cubicle, facing a screen, which shows his own face looking back at him.

The image on the screen is frozen, and of low resolution.

The door to the cubicle is clear glass, and behind it we can see the communication area of the Flight Deck – the Comms Center. In the Comms Center are Mace, Trey and Harvey. They are talking, but the glass door is fully soundproofed and we can't hear what they're saying.

Capa hits a button on the console in front of him, and the image on the screen begins to play.

CAPA

(*recording*)

Well. Mum and Dad. I hope you're proud of your son, saving mankind and so on. Don't be hard on big sis just because she isn't saving mankind. She's equally deserving of your love as me. (*Beat.*) Did I mention I was saving mankind?

He breaks off. The upbeat tone isn't right.

Capa deletes the message, and tries again.

Hi Mom. Hi Dad. (*Beat.*) By the time you get this message, I'll be in the dead zone. It came a little sooner than we thought. So you won't be able to send a message back. (*Beat.*) So I want to tell you: I don't need the message. I know everything you want to say.

Beat.

Capa stares into space.

Then deletes the message.

He tries a relaxed conversational tone.

Sis. Kiss the kids. Tell them their uncle said hi. And that I love them and stuff. Same goes for you too. (*Beat.*) Listen – are you taking Maxwell for a walk *every* day? Every day? At least forty-five minutes? Maxwell, if she isn't – bite her.

Cut to – Capa trying another tone.

I just want you to all know. There's nothing I'd rather be doing. There's no place I'd rather be.

Beat.

This sounds right to him.

He continues.

Just remember. It takes eight minutes for light to travel from the Sun to Earth. Which means you'll know if we succeeded about eight minutes after we deliver the payload. All you have to do is look out for a little extra brightness in the sky. And if you wake up one morning, and it's a particularly beautiful day . . . (*Shrugs.*) . . . you'll know we made it. (*Beat.*) Okay. I'm signing out. See you in a couple of years.

Capa presses send.

EXT. ICARUS II

Icarus II flies through space.

With an effect similar to Northern Lights, the glow of the solar wind kicks up and flickers around the hull.

INT. CORRIDOR

Corazon rides a scooter down the corridor, towards the Observation Room.

INT. OBSERVATION ROOM

Corazon enters the Observation Room.

It is extremely bright. She winces, shielding her eyes.

CORAZON

Icarus, dial it down a little, will you?

ICARUS

Yes, Corazon.

The light fades to a lower level, revealing something that was too bright to see previously . . .

Sitting on the observation couch is Captain Kaneda.

His eyes are wide, a little glazed. He looks almost in a trance.

CORAZON

. . . Captain?

Kaneda blinks, and rubs at his eyes.

I'm guessing you've been talking to Searle.

Kaneda looks towards Corazon, and seems to take a few moments to actually see her.

Then he finds his focus.

KANEDA

Did you send a package back?

CORAZON

I did. To my husband. You?

KANEDA

I said my goodbyes before I left.

CORAZON

I didn't realize I was saying goodbye.

Kaneda smiles.

KANEDA

So. Do you have that report for me?

CORAZON

Right here.

She hands Kaneda a printout, which he scans. As he reads:

The O2 productivity is good. In fact, if anything, we're over-producing. That will tail off dramatically when we get nearer. But in truth, we already have the oxygen reserves to make it there, and quarter-way back. (*Beat.*) You're thinking about *Icarus I*.

KANEDA

Always.

Corazon nods.

CORAZON

Well, whatever it was that tripped them up, I don't think it was lack of air. Not on the outward journey, at any rate.

INT. FLIGHT DECK/COMMS CENTER

Close up on the faces of Capa and Mace.

They are right next to each other, temples crushed together.

Both men are straining, teeth gritted, eyes blazing.

It takes a moment to realize they are fighting in the Communication Center.

Mace – much bigger and stronger than Capa – has Capa in a headlock.

Mace suddenly swings Capa around in a judo throw and slams him hard onto the floor.

Then he's on Capa, swinging his fist, punching Capa in the face . . .

Then he's being hauled off by Harvey and Trey.

TREY

Mace – what the hell are you doing?

MACE

(*struggling, yelling at Capa*)

Son of a bitch! Motherfucker!

Harvey and Trey pin Mace against the wall as Capa scrambles backwards.

HARVEY

Mace! Cut it out!

MACE

He took an hour in there! Now the wind is too high for me to send my package home!

CAPA

(*wiping blood off his mouth and nose*)

I'm sorry! I didn't realize I was taking so long!

INT. FLIGHT DECK

Cassie is on the Flight Deck.

The fight is going on within the Flight Deck area . . .

. . . but she is watching it on a live feed of the scene as Mace is held by Harvey and Trey, and Capa stands apart.

Cassie leans forwards and speaks into the comms link.

CASSIE

Kaneda. Searle. Report to Flight Deck.

KANEDA

(*over comms link*)

What's up?

Cassie glances at the live feed. It looks like a pub brawl on CCTV.

CASSIE

We have an excess of manliness breaking out in the Comms Center.

INT. MED CENTER

Mace sits opposite Searle.

Mace is nursing his knuckles in one hand, breathing hard.

Silence between the two men.

Eventually:

MACE

So how does this work?

Searle says nothing.

Am I supposed to tell you about my childhood?

Searle smiles.

SEARLE

I probably know more about your childhood than you do.

INT. SLEEPING QUARTERS/CAPTAIN'S QUARTERS

Kaneda sits in his Captain's quarters.

He's looking at a screen. On the screen, we can see it is a live feed from the Med Center, where Mace is talking to Searle.

Kaneda's face is blank, unreadable as he listens in on what Mace is saying . . .

MACE

Capa decides he doesn't want to cut his hair. Cassie reads the same book over and over. Kaneda stares at a chess board all day. You stare at the sun. Corazon talks to her plants. I fall asleep on duty. (*Beat.*) And get in a fist fight. (*Beat.*) Cause a fist fight. (*Beat.*) You'd think it was the pressure that would get to you. Everything riding on our shoulders. But it's not. It's the time. In sixteen months, you can get used to anything. (*Beat.*) You just . . . lose track. (*Beat.*) I know I screwed up.

Mace turns to look directly at the screen – and we realize he knows he is being watched.

From now on: I'm not losing track again.

Searle nods. Then types something on his desk keyboard.

SEARLE

Prescription. Earth Room. Two hours.

INT. MED CENTER/EARTH ROOM

Waves crash and thunder, and light catches the spray.

This image is projected on the walls, ceiling and floor of the Earth Room – a space of uncertain size, because the projected image hides the division between walls and floor.

It creates the impression that a person in the Earth Room is suspended in space.

In this instance: Mace.

A moment –

Then the sound and image of the waves vanishes and is replaced by –

Morning mist and soft light filtering through the leaves and branches of trees.

Mace frowns.

Mace reaches out – and puts his hand on the wall.

The wall is closer than we had thought.

MACE

. . . Bring the waves back.

ICARUS

Dr Searle's prescription specifies a peaceful module.

MACE

The waves make me feel peaceful.

A moment.

Then the waves return.

Outside the Earth Room, Searle watches.

INT. OXYGEN GARDEN

Capa sits alone in the Oxygen Garden, watching water collecting in the pool. His lip is split, but the cut is small and has dried over.

Mace enters.

Capa looks round.

A moment between them.

CAPA

Mace. I really am sorry. I should have let you go first, and . . .

MACE

(*cutting in*)

It's me. I'm the one apologizing, okay?

CAPA

. . . Okay.

Capa waits.

No apology comes.

Was that the apology?

MACE

(*uncomfortable*)

Yeah.

CAPA

. . . Consider it accepted.

MACE

Okay.

Mace exits, leaving Capa alone, somewhat bemused.

INT. FLIGHT DECK/COMMS CENTER

Harvey sits in the Comms Center.

In front of him, on his desk, running left to right, is a light beam, like a squared-off searchlight. It is a filtering device for sound: when Harvey puts his head into the light, interference is cancelled out, creating an exceptionally pure sound, or silence.

We can hear the fuzz sound of radio static.

But behind the static is another noise – looping, arcing tones and pitches.

This is the sound of the solar wind.

Harvey is checking through digital frequencies. The intensity of the static in relation to the solar wind varies, but neither can be cancelled entirely.

Harvey speaks into a microphone.

HARVEY

Icarus II to Moon Stations. This package timed at fifteen thirty-two, day four hundred and eighty-four, comms delay at five minutes and seventeen seconds. Total radio silence now for four hours and eleven minutes. Please respond.

Long beat – during which Harvey leans forwards into the light beam.

Immediately, the static cuts out, leaving only the solar wind.

Harvey listens for a few beats.

Then he pulls out, the static returns, and –

Icarus II to Moon Stations. This package timed at fifteen thirty-three, day four eighty-four, comms delay at five minutes and seventeen seconds. Total radio silence now for four hours and . . .

Harvey breaks off.

Twelve minutes.

Long beat. Harvey goes back into the light. Listens again.

Please respond.

Long beat.

(*Quiet.*) Okay. (*Beat.*) Moon Stations. This is Icarus II. Signing out.

Harvey remains in the light.

Listening to the solar wind.

The noise is strange, abstract but almost melodic.

EXT. ICARUS II

Hearing the solar wind, seeing the Northern Lights effect . . .

. . . through the window of the Oxygen Garden, where Corazon kneels by her plants . . .

EXT. ICARUS II

Hearing the solar wind in the Observation Room . . .

. . . where Searle sits, bathed in light.

INT. STELLAR BOMB/RAMP

Capa walks down a ramp which leads to a door. This is the entrance to the Stellar Bomb.

INT. STELLAR BOMB

Capa stands on a gantry, surrounded by darkness.

He is working on a console, his face is illuminated by the scrolling data.

INT. SLEEPING QUARTERS/CAPTAIN'S QUARTERS

Kaneda sits alone in his quarters, gazing at a video file that plays on his monitor.

The video file shows a corridor of Icarus I.

A man, Jim White, is speaking direct into camera.

Behind him we can see two other crew going about their business – a female crew member and Pinbacker.

Jim White is delivering a routine file report from Icarus I.

JIM WHITE
(*on video file*)
Water purification test passed okay. Radiation levels as expected.

In the background, the female crew member laughs.

JANE SPENCER
(*on video file*)
He means: our cell replication process is totally out of control.

Jim White continues.

JIM WHITE

(*on video file*)

Recommend delay to centrifuge test, until we've finished the diagnostic on the release panel. I'll deal with that myself as soon as we're clear of this cycle.

Kaneda hits a button. Skips to the next report.

PINBACKER

(*on video file*)

It was a sequence of contact reports on the top-left shield quadrant, which, by seventeen hundred, Moon Time, had turned into a minor asteroid storm. None bigger than a raindrop, but we had nineteen punctures and a secondary contact to the engine compartment. Took us three alpha shifts to patch it up. Lost a little vapor. Not serious.

Pinbacker pauses.

I watched them hit us from the O2 garden. Got to tell you, Moon Base: it was beautiful.

Kaneda hits pause. He rubs his eyes. He's been doing this for hours.

On the monitor screen, Pinbacker's face is frozen.

INT. FLIGHT DECK

Cassie sits in the co-pilot's seat.

Her dog-eared copy of Lady Chatterley's Lover *is face down on her lap, folded open about two-thirds through the text.*

But she isn't reading.

She has seen something.

In front of her is a wide portal screen, similar to the portal to the Observation Room, but this is cluttered with the symbols and readings of a heads-up display.

CASSIE

Wow.

On the cluttered screen, we can't make out what she has seen.

And behind her, neither Mace nor Trey looks up. They are engrossed in calculations and readings.

Guys. You want to see something?

INT. CORRIDOR/OUTSIDE OBSERVATION ROOM

Outside the Observation Room, all the scooters are parked.

INT. OBSERVATION ROOM

The entire crew is gathered in the Observation Room.

TREY

Speech!

CAPA

Speech!

SEARLE

Oh, all right. I did have a few words I wanted to say.

Everyone laughs . . .

. . . because the guy who has to make a speech is Kaneda.

Kaneda walks to the front of the room, with the vast and darkened view window behind him.

Kaneda takes a moment.

KANEDA

Well – I *should* have a few words to say . . . but on reflection, what can one say?

He pauses for effect.

Then:

Ladies and gentlemen . . .

The view window brightens.

Mercury.

Revealed, behind him, the stunning vision of . . .

. . . Mercury, eclipsing the Sun, which burns in a penumbra around the silhouetted planet.

A black disc and a burning halo.

EXT. MERCURY

Stunning views of the Sun-blasted planet . . .

. . . in space . . .

. . . illuminated by the Sun . . .

. . . then Mercury and Icarus II and the Sun behind.

INT. FLIGHT DECK/COMMS CENTER

Harvey sits in his chair, dozing with his chin on his chest. We notice he has a few days' stubble showing.

Over the speakers is the sound of the solar winds.

EXT. MERCURY

The shadow of Icarus II races across the surface of the Sun-blasted planet.

As the shadow reaches Mercury's dark side, cut back to –

INT. FLIGHT DECK/COMMS CENTER

– Harvey. Through the sound of the solar winds, we hear:

Faintly, a steady series of regularly spaced tones. On, off, on, off.

Close-up on Harvey's face.

Eyes opening. Reacting.

INT. SOCIAL AREA

A meting has been called. Capa, Mace, Cassie, Corazon and Trey sit in the briefing area.

We notice that:

Capa's beard and hair are longer, and he is more bedraggled.

Mace has cut his hair very short.

Corazon has earth and dirt embedded under her fingernails, into her fingerprints.

Kaneda enters, followed by Searle and Harvey.

Searle is wearing sunglasses with extremely dark black-out lenses, and his skin is reddened and peeling slightly.

Kaneda waits while Searle and Harvey take their seats . . .

KANEDA

Okay.

Kaneda takes another moment as they settle.

Okay – here it is. (*Beat.*) I've put us into orbit around Mercury.

The crew, excepting Harvey and Searle, exchange puzzled glances.

I've done this in case we want to change our exit from the planet's gravity.

More puzzled glances.

You will also be aware that we have now been out of communication with Moon Stations for fifty-six days.

CASSIE

Captain, I'm not following. Why would we want to alter our trajectory?

Kaneda turns to Harvey.

KANEDA

Harvey – you want to pick this up?

Harvey nods.

HARVEY

Twenty-three hours ago, while making a routine check of the comms systems . . .

MACE

(*dry*)

While listening to your space music.

Harvey ignores this.

HARVEY

. . . while scanning the frequencies, I heard a transmission.

All react – including Mace.

HARVEY

It appeared as we flew into the dark side of Mercury. The iron content of the planet is acting as an antennae. There's still high background interference, but the signal is clear enough. (*Beat.*) Icarus. Please play audio file seven-five forward-slash B.

ICARUS

Yes, Harvey.

Over the speaker system, the audio file begins to play.

As before, we hear the regularly spaced tones come through the static and solar wind.

HARVEY

End file.

The audio file stops.

MACE

What is it?

HARVEY

It's the Icarus I. And that sound is their distress beacon.

Stunned silence in the Briefing Room. Then:

CASSIE

Jesus.

TREY

It's impossible. It's been seven years . . .

HARVEY

(*cutting in*)

It's clearly not impossible because you can hear the beacon with your own ears.

CASSIE

Are you saying they're alive?

KANEDA

We don't know.

CORAZON

But we know that they could be.

All eyes on Corazon.

Their oxygen is self-replenishing. Water is recycled. They have all the solar power they need.

MACE

What about food? No way their supplies could have lasted seven years.

Kaneda speaks again.

KANEDA

That depends. They had stock to cover eight people for three years.

MACE

That's a four-year shortfall. Hell of a diet.

KANEDA

Only if you're feeding eight. We don't know what happened to Icarus I. There might have been an accident. Or something else. There might not have been eight people to feed.

A beat.

Then Capa speaks for the first time.

CAPA

I have a question.

KANEDA

Yes.

CAPA

Do we know where they are?

A glance between Kaneda and Searle.

SEARLE

Well done, Capa. That is *the* question.

The monitor screen behind Kaneda lights up, to show a graphic of:

The Sun, Mercury and Icarus II.

KANEDA

Icarus. Please plot our trajectory following the sling shot around Mercury.

The trajectory appears.

Now plot the source of the Icarus I beacon.

An icon appears between Mercury and the Sun. It is near to – but not on – the trajectory course. And it is extremely close to the Sun . . .

CAPA

(*stunned*)

Jesus. They so nearly made it.

KANEDA

It's why no one picked up the signal until now. It was lost in the background light and noise.

CASSIE

(*quiet*)

We're going to pass right by them.

KANEDA

Within ten or fifteen thousand miles.

CORAZON

We'll be able to see them.

KANEDA

Yes.

Cassie's eyes suddenly well up.

TREY

But . . .

SEARLE

(*quick*)

What?

TREY

Well – I'd need to look at all of this pretty carefully. Very carefully. But . . . if I had to make a guess right now . . . (*Takes a deep breath.*) I'd say we could adjust our trajectory. We could fly straight to them.

MACE

(fast, firm)

But. We are not going to.

All eyes on Mace.

Just to make it clear. There is absolutely no way we are going to do that.

All eyes still on Mace.

What? You want me to spell it out? We have a payload to deliver to the heart of our nearest star. We are delivering that payload because the star is dying. And if it dies, we all die. Everything dies. So that is our mission. And there is nothing – literally *nothing* – more important than completing the mission. End of story.

TREY

He's right.

MACE

'He's right'? Of course I'm 'right'. Is anyone here seriously thinking otherwise?

He scans the faces in front of him. And clearly, some of them are.

SEARLE

May I put a counter-argument?

MACE

No!

SEARLE

Captain?

KANEDA

Go ahead.

SEARLE

It would, of course, be absurd to alter our trajectory to assist the crew of the Icarus I. Even if we knew that some or even all of the crew were still alive, their lives are entirely expendable when seen in the context of our mission. As are our own lives.

MACE

Exactly!

SEARLE

However. There is something on the Icarus I that may be worth the detour. As you pointed out, Mace, we have a payload to deliver. 'A' payload, singular. And everything about the delivery and effectiveness of that payload is entirely theoretical. Simply put, we don't know if it's going to work. But what we do know is this. (*Beat.*) If we had *two* payloads, we would have two chances.

Silence.

HARVEY

You're assuming we'd be able to pilot Icarus I.

SEARLE

Yes.

TREY

Which is assuming that whatever stopped them completing the mission wasn't a fault or damage to the spacecraft.

SEARLE

Yes.

MACE

That's a *lot* of assumptions.

SEARLE

It is. It's a risk assessment. The question is, does the risk of the detour outweigh the benefits of an extra payload?

Mace glances around the table.

Cassie's eyes are shining with tears for the crew of Icarus I.

Harvey, Trey and Corazon are with Mace.

Kaneda is unreadable.

Searle is behind shades.

Capa is undecided.

MACE

We'll have a vote.

SEARLE

No. We won't. We aren't a democracy. We're a collection of astronauts and scientists. So we will make the most informed decision available to us.

MACE

Made by you, by any chance?

KANEDA

Made by the person best qualified to understand the complexities of the payload delivery. Our physicist.

All look to Capa.

We particularly notice: Cassie watching Capa.

CAPA

(*under his breath*)

Shit.

INT. SOCIAL AREA

Time-lapse of the crew leaving, except Capa, until –

Capa is alone in the social area.

He is sat at the table.

Attached to the wall is a small basketball hoop – a toy, for a ball no larger than a tennis ball.

In Capa's hand is the mini-basketball.

He throws it at the hoop.

It hits the rim, and bounces out.

The ball rolls back towards Capa.

He watches it, blank-faced, as it comes to a rest by his feet.

INT. CAPA'S BUNK

Capa lies in his bunk, frosted privacy-partition pulled down.

He is wide awake, staring at the ceiling just a metre above his nose.

Attached to the ceiling is a hologram photo of his pet dog, Maxwell.

On the frame of the hologram photo is a single red button.

Capa presses it.

Noiselessly, Maxwell barks and wags his tail.

INT. MED CENTER/EARTH ROOM

Capa stands in the Earth Room. He is alone, and surrounded by a strange projection.

In front of him is the planet Earth – and we are orbiting.

Orbiting fast, because every few moments the Moon slides by, behind the Earth. Followed moments later by the Sun . . .

. . . which gives the projection a very slow strobe.

As a constant in front of him, a spaceship is being built in time-lapse. Smaller spacecraft swarm like crew around a Formula One car at a pit-stop.

As the ship takes shape, we realize it is Icarus, and as its name appears on the side, we realize it is Icarus I.

We continue until Icarus I is completed, and then, with a flare of boosters, the ship launches towards its destination.

We follow the ship at a vastly accelerated pace, powering through the colossal expanses of space, seeing as it first slingshots the Moon . . .

Then Venus, then Mercury . . .

Until it is blazing towards the Sun.

Meanwhile, Capa stands, hypnotized, or transfixed, deep in concentration.

ICARUS

Capa. We are now passing the position from which the distress beacon is being transmitted.

CAPA

Affirmative, Icarus. Continue the animatic.

ICARUS

Yes, Capa. But please be aware that –

CAPA

(*cuts in*)

I know. Continue as long as you can.

As Capa talks, the animatic begins to play in line with his description.

CAPA

Detach the payload.

Beat.

Four minutes after separation, boosters automatically fire . . .

The boosters fire.

The ship continues its descent towards the Sun.

Then – abruptly – a distortion passes across the payload section of the spaceship. Then it flickers, then slows, then speeds up, then freezes.

The payload is frozen just as it is about to contact the surface of the Sun.

ICARUS

Reliability of projection has dropped below forty-five percent. Remaining projection is not open to useful speculation. Variables infinite. Accuracy unknown.

Beat.

CAPA

Yeah.

Capa nods.

That is the problem, right there.

Capa has directed this comment over his shoulder, at *someone.*

For the first time we realize that Capa is not alone in the Earth Room. Kaneda is leaning against the back wall, behind Capa, watching with arms crossed.

Between the boosters and the gravity of the sun, the velocity of the payload will be so great that space and time will become smeared together. Everything will distort. Everything will be unquantifiable.

Silence.

KANEDA

You have to come down on one side or the other. I need a decision.

CAPA

It's not a decision. It's a guess. It's like flipping a coin, and asking me to make a decision about whether it'll be heads or tails.

KANEDA

And?

Capa shrugs.

CAPA

Heads.

Silence again.

Capa lets himself drift off again. For a moment, he has lost himself in the surrounding incandescence.

Then he turns to Kaneda.

There isn't going to be another payload, so the one we carry is our last chance. Our last best hope. (*Beat.*) Searle's argument is sound. Two last hopes are better than one.

KANEDA

Okay. (*Nods.*) That's it.

Cut to:

EXT. ICARUS II

Icarus II, flying fast away from the planet Mercury.

EXT. THE SUN

The surface of the Sun.

INT. SLEEPING QUARTERS/CAPA'S BUNK

Capa lies asleep.

The partition to his bunk opens.

It's Cassie.

She looks down on him for several moments – then sits on the bed beside him.

For several moments Capa remains asleep, then – intuition that he is not alone – he wakes.

And sees her.

CAPA
(*slightly puzzled*)
Hey.

CASSIE
Hey.

Capa rubs the sleep out of his eyes.

Good dream? (*Beat.*) Let me guess. The surface of the sun.

Capa doesn't confirm this. But we know she's right.

It's the only dream I ever have. Every time I shut my eyes, always the same.

CAPA
Maybe you should talk to Searle about that.

Cassie smiles.

CASSIE
Maybe. (*Beat.*) I just wanted to let you know. I think you made the right choice.

CAPA
Mace doesn't. And I'm guessing Harvey and Trey don't either.

Cassie shrugs.

CASSIE
But I do.

Cut to:

INT. SLEEPING QUARTERS

Darkness in the sleeping quarters. A sense that this is the night shift.

Suddenly an alarm is sounding.

MACE

(*over intercom*)

All crew report immediately to Flight Deck.

A frozen beat – then partitions are opening, people are scrambling out of bed, and running for the Flight Deck.

INT. FLIGHT DECK

All arrive at the Flight Deck, to find Mace and Trey checking a hologram schematic of the Icarus II.

KANEDA

What's going on?

TREY

(*ashen-faced*)

I screwed up.

MACE

It's not you who screwed up.

TREY

It's my responsibility.

MACE

If we weren't straying from the mission –

KANEDA

(*firm*)

Trey – cut to it.

TREY

In order to change the route, I had to manually override Icarus. So I made all the calculations myself. And I double- and triple-checked them. They all worked out, so I set the new coordinates and . . . put us on our way.

KANEDA

So what's the problem? The trajectory is wrong?

Trey swallows nervously.

TREY

The trajectory is good. But it changes our angle of approach to the Sun by one point one degrees.

And Capa is a step ahead.

CAPA

You didn't reset the shields to the new angle.

A beat.

HARVEY

Jesus Christ, Trey.

All eyes on Trey.

TREY

I . . .

Trey breaks off as if he can hardly believe the answer himself.

Then, helplessly:

. . . I forgot.

Silence.

(*Stammering.*) My . . . head was full of velocities and fuel calculations, and a million different . . . (*Snapping, freaking out.*) I forgot, all right? It happens! People do shit! They get stressed and they fuck up! And I fucked up!

Kaneda steps in.

KANEDA

(*taking control*)

Enough! Everyone take a moment! Trey. The fact is, we're still alive. A hole hasn't burned in the side of the ship, and we don't have a ten-thousand-degree climate. So how bad is this? What's the actual damage?

Behind Mace is the hologram schematic.

MACE

We don't know. Icarus tried to reset the shield independently when the alarm triggered. But all the sensors up there burned out, so we have no idea of the state of the affected area. (*Beat.*) The only way we're going to know is to go out there.

A moment.

KANEDA

Okay. I'll get suited up.

HARVEY

It's a two-man job.

KANEDA

As Second in Command, you're not going anywhere.

TREY

I volunteer.

MACE

(*firm*)

No. I volunteer.

KANEDA

Fine.

MACE

I volunteer Capa.

A moment.

Capa looks over at Mace, who meets the gaze completely straight and even.

CAPA

Sure.

Capa's courage is betrayed by the trickle of sweat that escapes his hairline.

I'll do it.

INT. AIRLOCK

Kaneda and Capa suit up.

Every part of the suit is made of a strange, mirrored material – every surface reflects, causing strange distortions where the stiff suit material is rippled or folded.

We can see it is impossible to put the suits on alone. The suits are too bulky and awkward in the gravity of the spaceship.

It is necessary to be assisted.

Cassie is helping Capa, and Harvey is helping Kaneda.

CASSIE

You've been through this a thousand times in Earth-orbit training.

CAPA

(*tight, scared*)

Yeah.

CASSIE

You're going to be fine.

Capa nods.

He's looking straight into Cassie's eyes as . . .

Clunk.

The heavy mirrored helmet is dropped over Capa's head and a suck of pressurized air locks the rim into place . . .

. . . leaving a reflection of Cassie's face where Capa's had been.

Cassie locks the helmet into place by putting her hand on both sides of the helmet and pulling down sharply, activating locking clasps around the neck-ring.

INT. FLIGHT DECK

Cassie sits in the pilot's seat, with Corazon and Harvey standing behind.

Mace sits in the engineer's seat. Trey sits at the navigation table.

CASSIE

Okay, Icarus. I'm going to be taking control here for a while.

ICARUS

Yes, Cassie.

CASSIE

I'm going to be cutting speed. Then I'm going to be rotating us so that the damaged area is facing away from the sun. Do we understand each other?

ICARUS

Yes, Cassie.

HARVEY

If you rotate by that much, we're going to lose the comms towers.

MACE

Good job we don't need them, then.

HARVEY

We don't need them now. We'll need them on the way home.

CASSIE

And we'll cross that bridge when we come to it. In the meantime, I'm going to give them as much shadow as I can.

Close up on Trey's face as Cassie says:

Please adjust shields to allow for the rotation.

Trey closes his eyes.

EXT. ICARUS II

The whole of Icarus II rotates slowly.

An amazing sight as:

. . . the ship rotates, and the mirrored scales on the shield ripple, all moving independently, directing themselves to best reflect the Sun's blaze.

INT. FLIGHT DECK

The crew on the Flight Deck falls silent as the ship begins to echo with strange noises.

Oddly like whale song – groans and clicks: the reverberating sounds of stressed and twisting metal.

CORAZON

Jesus.

MACE

It's the temperature change on the shields. The metal is contracting and expanding.

CORAZON

I know what it is, fly-boy.

A series of clicks like hammer blows ripples through the ship.

Instinctively, Corazon rests a hand on the console.

It just sounds like she's tearing apart.

EXT. ICARUS II

As the ship turns, light hits the comms towers.

Parts of the towers burn away at once. A beam of light reflects off the part of the comms towers that remains.

ICARUS

Fatal damage to comms towers three and four.

INT. AIRLOCK

Kaneda and Capa are alone in the airlock, fully suited.

MACE

(*over radio link*)

Okay. I'm opening up.

KANEDA

We're set.

The airlock opens to outer space.

EXT. ICARUS II

Kaneda and Capa emerge from the airlock.

All conversation is heard over radio links.

KANEDA

Kaneda, check, helmet-cam fully operational.

INT. FLIGHT DECK

The hull vanishes to show two images – live feeds from cameras on the helmets of Kaneda and Capa.

MACE

Affirmative. Good image.

CAPA

(over radio link)

Capa, check, helmet-cam operational.

MACE

Affirmative.

KANEDA

(over radio link)

Okay. Moving down to investigate damaged area.

EXT. ICARUS II

Kaneda and Capa move down Icarus II, away from the airlock . . .

Then trigger their jetpacks, and begin the long journey towards the edge of the shield.

EXT. ICARUS II/SHIELD

Kaneda and Capa peer over the edge of the shield.

In the shadowed area, they can see a vast field of the slightly tilted scale panels.

Then they move over to the control box for that section.

Kaneda opens the box up.

Inside, we can see scorch marks from blown circuits.

KANEDA

Can you guys see this?

MACE
(*over radio link*)
We see it.

KANEDA
The relay is burned out. Give me a moment.

Kaneda pulls out the section of fused circuitry within the control box.

Capa hands him the replacement, and Kaneda fits it.

KANEDA
Okay, Mace. Test it.

A moment later, a beautiful ripple as the field of slightly upright panels drop to a position which is flush with the larger curve form of the shield.

All panels save four. A cluster, a long way distant from the edge of the shield where the two suited men stand.

KANEDA
(*quiet*)
Shit.

A beat.

KANEDA
Mace, try it again.

The panels all lift to their previous slightly tilted position . . .

. . . then drop again.

And again, the four panels are locked in half-upright positions.

CAPA
The hydraulics have gone. We're lucky Icarus caught it in time to prevent a hull breach.

KANEDA
Agreed. (*He sighs.*) Okay. Looks like we're going out there.

EXT. ICARUS II

We watch from a distance as Capa and Kaneda make their way across the large distance to the damaged hydraulics.

EXT. ICARUS II/SHIELD

Kaneda moves over to one of the four half-upright scales – which gives us a clear sense of proportion of the size of the ship, as the scale is twice as tall as he is – and takes out a tool from a utility pouch on his suit.

Like everything else, the tool is perfectly mirrored on every surface.

Capa watches as Kaneda works on the scale.

Kaneda cuts or releases something in the hydraulics.

The scale moves to a fully upright position.

This allows Kaneda to manoeuvre the bulky space suit to reach the mechanism underneath.

He works inside . . .

. . . then Kaneda pushes himself backwards as, slowly, the huge scale begins to return to the side of Icarus II.

KANEDA

Mace. Head for my quarters and check the bottom drawer. You'll find a bottle of champagne.

MACE

(*over radio link*)

You can do it?

KANEDA

It'll take a while, but – yeah. We can do it.

Over radio link – the sound of cheering.

All right, Capa. You set 'em up, and I'll knock 'em down.

EXT. ICARUS II

The Sun and solar-wind blasted view of Icarus II.

And we see that now, as the gravity centrifuge of the ship turns . . .

. . . light reflected off the damaged comms tower is striking the mirrored glass of the Oxygen Garden portal.

And each time it does so, beneath the portal, the plants are bathed in bleaching light.

INT. OXYGEN GARDEN

Bright sunlight hits the pool of water.

A coil of steam rises.

INT. FLIGHT DECK

Cassie and Mace are watching the Kaneda and Capa helmet-cams – where Kaneda and Capa are close to completing their task.

On the monitors we can see that there are three frozen scales remaining.

Two have been made fully upright by Capa, and one is still half-upright.

Corazon is in front of a separate panel which shows oxygen consumption.

There are three boxes on the panel. One for each space suit, and one for Icarus. And in each box is a simple numerical readout.

Corazon is watching Capa's consumption figures, which are falling more rapidly than Kaneda's.

CORAZON

Capa – take it easy. You're going through your O2 pretty fast.

CAPA

(*over comms link*)

Copy that, Cory.

CORAZON

That's it. Slow down the breathing. Relaxed movement.

Corazon does not seem to have noticed that the consumption figures for Icarus have started to move even faster than Capa's . . .

. . . and they seem to be gaining speed.

HARVEY

(*into comms link*)

Good work, guys.

Mace glances back to Trey at the navigation table.

MACE

Trey. Stop killing yourself. We've got this . . .

He is cut off as the alarm starts to sound.

All freeze a moment. Then Mace hits a button and the alarm stops.

CASSIE

Icarus?

ICARUS

Resuming computer control of Icarus II.

Mace and Cassie exchange a glance.

CASSIE

Negative, Icarus. Manual control.

The numbers of Icarus's oxygen consumption are moving faster.

ICARUS

Negative, Cassie. Computer control. Returning vessel to original rotation.

MACE

What the hell?

CASSIE

Icarus – override computer control to manual.

ICARUS

Negative.

In front of Corazon, the consumption numbers suddenly start to move at the speed of the decimal numbers on a stop watch.

And now Corazon sees them.

CORAZON

. . . Oh shit. I think we're venting O2.

KANEDA

(*over radio link*)

What's going on here, guys? We're moving . . .

ICARUS

Mission in jeopardy. Override command statement. Manual flight controls removed.

CASSIE

Negative, Icarus! *Negative!* State reason *immediately*!

The picture on the monitors changes from the helmet-cams to show a weird and freakish image. A jungle enveloped in a raging blaze.

INT. OXYGEN GARDEN

An intense fire rages in the garden.

ICARUS

Fire in Oxygen Garden.

EXT. ICARUS II

Capa moves away as the last half-upright scale is released and moves to the fully upright position.

He looks around and watches as Icarus II slowly rotates . . .

And sees . . .

. . . as the ship is rotating, the area taking the full impact of the Sun and solar-winds is moving around to their position.

INT. FLIGHT DECK

Chaos on the Flight Deck. Cassie, Mace and Harvey are running through procedure, working the consoles . . .

. . . as Corazon heads for the door.

HARVEY

Seal oxygen sector. Seal oxygen feed.

MACE

Fireguard perimeter. Seal sectors five through nine.

CASSIE

Perimeter, check. Sectors five through nine, check.

HARVEY

Rerouting coolant to O2 storage tanks.

CASSIE

Check. Mace – boost water pressure to oxygen sector.

MACE

I'm on it.

INT. CORRIDOR TO OXYGEN GARDEN

Corazon is heading towards the Oxygen Garden.

INT. FLIGHT DECK

CASSIE

(*into radio-mike*)

Kaneda! Capa! Get back to the airlock *now*!

TREY

They're going to die. They're going to burn up.

CASSIE

They are *not*! Override Icarus – Cassie, pilot, emergency command zero-zero-zero.

ICARUS

Copy command zero-zero-zero. Second human confirmation required.

CASSIE

Copy. Mace.

Mace says nothing. He's frowning, thinking fast.

CASSIE

Mace!

MACE

Wait, Cassie. I . . .

CASSIE

(*cuts in*)

Harvey! For Christ's sake!

Harvey's gaze flicks at Mace – then Cassie.

HARVEY

Harvey. Comms Officer. Confirm back-up, zero-zero-zero.

ICARUS

Override command confirmed. Manual control returned. Warning. Warning. Mission in fatal compromise.

. . . *Now back to Mace – motionless in the chaos, detached.*

He's now thought it through.

MACE

No.

Mace speaks quietly – but it cuts through the commotion.

MACE

Icarus – continue procedure.

CASSIE

. . . What?

MACE

(*into comms link*)

Captain. Back me up.

KANEDA

(*over comms link*)

Copy, Mace. Kaneda, Captain. Override control alpha one. Icarus – take control.

ICARUS

Affirmative.

CASSIE

(*quiet*)

Oh Jesus.

EXT. ICARUS II

Comparative stillness outside the vessel.

Then – at a graceful speed, the ship starts to rotate again.

CAPA

Captain.

KANEDA

Can't.

Kaneda is working fast, but his voice is calm.

Can't leave upright panels. Certain hull breach.

Capa starts working on the panel he just got to the upright position.

Silence between the two men.

Broken intermittently by snatched broadcasts over the radio link.

CASSIE

The fire is out of control.

MACE

I've got failure lights everywhere. Where's the fucking back-up?

HARVEY

Burned out. It's all burned out.

CASSIE

Icarus – I need a hazard diagnostic.

MACE

Fuck! Fuck it!

And through these shouts, the sound of Corazon screaming.

INT. CORRIDOR/OUTSIDE OXYGEN GARDEN

Corazon stands in the glass corridor leading into the Oxygen Garden, crying out at the sight of her garden burning.

Water from the sprinkler system is raining down . . .

. . . but the fire is too intense. It is making no impact.

Half the garden is now ablaze.

ICARUS

Sprinkler system failing.

CORAZON

Let me in!

ICARUS

Negative. Door sealed by operating superior Comms Officer.

CORAZON

Harvey, you motherfucker! *Let me in!*

INT. FLIGHT DECK

ICARUS

Hazard diagnostic complete. Fire will burn for six hours. Sixty percent chance of containment failure. Seventy-five percent chance of collateral damage to life-support systems . . .

HARVEY

(*edge of panic*)

What are we going to do?

But Mace is still calm.

MACE

Remove gravity. Flood the garden with O2.

HARVEY

. . . What?

MACE

It will cause a flash over. Make it burn itself out.

CASSIE

We'll lose the whole garden.

MACE

We've lost it already.

HARVEY

Jesus, Mace. I don't know . . .

MACE

Icarus – remove gravity. Engineer override.

He looks to Cassie.

Beat.

CASSIE

Pilot. Override confirmed.

EXT. ICARUS II

The rotation of Icarus II starts to slow.

INT. CORRIDOR/OUTSIDE OXYGEN GARDEN

Sudden new alarm on Corazon's face . . .

. . . as zero gravity starts to take effect.

CORAZON

No!

Her feet lift off the ground . . .

No! We can fight it! *We can fight it!*

INT. OXYGEN GARDEN

An amazing sequence . . .

As zero gravity takes effect, the fire in the garden loses convection relating to up or down.

The fire begins to radiate out in all directions, as if shining.

Within twenty seconds, the entire garden is burning in the weird and intense blaze.

INT. CORRIDOR/OUTSIDE OXYGEN GARDEN

In the glass corridor, Corazon is suddenly engulfed in smoke.

EXT. ICARUS II

Silence again, as Capa and Kaneda work on their respective panels.

At the same moment, both Capa and Kaneda's panels start to move back to the down position . . .

Leaving only one remaining.

Both move towards it.

Kaneda is nearer. He gets there first.

Capa looks back over his shoulder.

The solar wind and sunlight is moving closer . . .

KANEDA
(*not looking round*)

Go.

CAPA

Captain.

KANEDA

Go.

Capa still doesn't move.

Silence.

Then Capa starts to head back.

We follow Capa . . .

In silence, back across the vast shield.

As Capa travels, the rotating section of Icarus II starts to move again.

When Capa reaches the edge of the shield, he looks back and sees . . .

Kaneda moving away from the panel, as it starts to drop to the down position.

Kaneda turns towards Capa.

The two men face each other across the great distance.

Kaneda doesn't move. The sunlight is too close, moving too fast, and the distance he would have to travel is too far. He knows it is pointless.

Cut to:

INT. FLIGHT DECK

Mace, Cassie, Harvey, frozen, watching the monitor image of Kaneda's head-cam.

CASSIE

He's not going to make it.

HARVEY

(*quiet*)

He's switched off his audio.

Trey can't watch. One look at his face tells us he is putting all responsibility for the catastrophe on his own shoulders.

Cut to:

EXT. ICARUS II

Kaneda waits motionless as the sunlight and solar winds move towards him.

Cut to:

INT. MED CENTER

Searle watching the helmet-cam on a monitor in the Med Center.

Searle is an extremely strange sight. He isn't wearing the black-lens sunglasses, and where the sunglasses would be his skin is pale white. But the rest of his face is badly sunburned, red, peeling.

SEARLE

(*whispers*)

Kaneda. (*Intense.*) What can you see?

INT. INSIDE KANEDA'S HELMET

Kaneda's face as he watches the sunlight get closer.

SEARLE

(*over radio link*)

What can you see?

EXT. ICARUS II

The sunlight has almost reached Kaneda. It's only a metre away.

He could reach out and touch it . . .

. . . and he does.

His hand lifts, moves into the area of light, and is immediately ignited like a magnesium strip.

Kaneda keeps his hand there, staring at fingers that glow like light-bulb filaments, impossibly bright.

EXT. ICARUS II/SHIELD

From the edge of the shield, Capa watches as the sunlight takes Kaneda.

KANEDA

(*faint, over radio link*)

Oh God.

The link cuts.

EXT. ICARUS II

Kaneda's whole figure is blazing with the white-hot brightness.

You can hardly tell the figure was ever a man. In seconds, the fierce glow has burned away entirely, and absolutely nothing of Kaneda remains.

EXT. ICARUS II/SHIELD

Capa watches as long as he can . . .

. . . then ducks down, just as the sunlight reaches the edge of the shield.

Fade to:

INT. MED CENTER

Trey lies in the Med Center.

He is attached to a drip, apparently in a drug-induced coma.

Over this, we hear Harvey's voice.

HARVEY

(*voice-over*)

The breakdown is as follows. As Second in Command, I am now the captain of Icarus II. (*Beat.*) Trey is sedated in the Med Center. Dr Searle has diagnosed him as a suicide risk. I don't think any of us are about to question that diagnosis.

INT. SOCIAL AREA

All crew except Trey are in the Briefing Area.

Harvey continues in his breakdown of their situation.

Note: throughout, Searle is picking and pulling at his sunburned forearm, tugging off long strips of dead skin.

HARVEY

Thanks to both Kanada and Capa, our shields are intact. As is the payload. We don't have a problem there.

Harvey lets that sink in a moment before the bombshell.

But the Oxygen Garden is totally destroyed. In addition, a large amount of O2 was burned in the fire. As it stands now, we do not have enough reserves to get us to our payload delivery point. (*Beat.*) Let alone to survive the return journey.

Silence. Broken by Mace.

MACE

So cancel the ticker-tape parade.

Capa looks at Mace. Mace doesn't look at Capa.

HARVEY

We now have no choice but to rendezvous with Icarus I. There remains the possibility that the ship is largely intact. There is a secondary possibility that we could salvage what is left of their garden. (*Beat.*) If we're going to survive the mission, the Icarus I is now our only hope.

EXT. ICARUS II

Icarus II flying through space.

INT. OXYGEN GARDEN

The plants are all burned to blackened stumps and ashes.

Water drifts down from the sprinkler system like rain.

Corazon is setting up work lights, which reveal the devastation as they are illuminated.

INT. PAYLOAD AIRLOCK/INTERSECTION

Searle walks through the airlock that leads to the Payload Bay.

INT. STELLAR BOMB/RAMP

On Searle –

Pull back to reveal that he is walking across a vast flat plane. The huge space is completely at odds with the otherwise cramped confines of the ship.

We are seeing one surface of the Stellar Bomb – a colossal mirrored cube, whose size we have never been able to appreciate until now. The small figure of Searle on its topside is dwarfed by the scale.

Searle walks towards a ramp, in the center of the bomb's top surface, which leads down to the bomb's interior.

INT. STELLAR BOMB

Searle enters.

He walks onto a gantry.

Above, beside and below is only blackness – with no indication of size or dimension. From visual evidence, the space could stretch an infinite distance, and feels as if it does.

At the end of the gantry is a console, on which Capa stands, reading data streams that illuminate his face.

SEARLE

So it doesn't look as if we're going home.

Capa says nothing.

How do you feel about that?

CAPA

Do you mean: how do I feel about us dying in space, or how I feel about it being my responsibility?

SEARLE

Either.

CAPA

How do you feel about it?

A beat.

SEARLE

Unsurprised. Perhaps I never imagined this as a two-way trip.

CAPA

What about the rest of the crew?

SEARLE

I don't know how they feel.

CAPA

You're going around each of us, doing a quick psych-test. An assessment. Finding out if any of us are going to lose our shit. You know how they feel.

Searle smiles.

SEARLE

You were first on my list.

Silence.

Then Capa turns to face Searle.

CAPA

The truth?

SEARLE

Of course.

Capa turns back to vast blackness of the payload.

CAPA

This space has dark matter of equal mass to the moon, compressed into a space the size of a football stadium.

As he talks, he illustrates this by taking something from his pocket. We recognize it at once: the silver king from Kaneda's chess set.

Enough mass to create its own gravity.

Capa throws the silver king towards Searle.

From its flight – at one-sixth normal speed – we can see the gravity effect that Capa describes.

CAPA

Within the space, at our command, a single spark will pop into existence. Then that spark will split in two. Then those two will split again. And again. And again. And before you know it . . . (*Beat.*) A reaction that generates more energy than it consumes. A Big Bang on a small scale.

Finishing its arc through the air, the chess piece lands gently in Searle's palm.

A glimpse at the dawn of time. (*Beat.*) I think it will be beautiful.

SEARLE

I think so too.

Silence.

CAPA

I'd like to see it. (*Beat.*) I can live with not going home.

Searle places the silver king on the console.

INT. SOCIAL AREA

Corazon, Mace and Cassie are all in the mess.

Capa, Harvey, Trey and Searle are absent.

Corazon has something she wants to say, but is finding it hard to find the right words.

When she speaks, it is quietly, as if not wanting her voice to carry too far.

CORAZON

Technically, he made a mistake.

MACE

Spit it out, Cory.

CORAZON

Harvey said there's not enough oxygen to get us to the payload delivery point. But there is. (*Beat.*) There just isn't enough oxygen to get *all* of us there.

Corazon lets this sink in.

I'm not *recommending* anything.

A moment.

MACE

You aren't suggesting we let Trey kill himself.

CORAZON

No! (*Beat.*) And in any case . . . Trey wouldn't be enough. (*Beat.*) We'd need to lose two more.

Mace raises his eyebrows.

MACE

Three out of seven. That's a lot of short straws.

CORAZON

Like I said. I'm not recommending anything. I just thought people should know.

INT. CASSIE'S BUNK

Cassie lies in her bunk, asleep.

Dreaming – disturbed – about the surface of the Sun.

Until she wakes with a start.

INT. ICARUS MAINFRAME

Mace is working in the mainframe, with steam rolling out of his mouth in the freezing air.

He is using a spanner-like tool in an awkward position. He's not concentrating. Corazon's words are playing and replaying in his mind.

His hand slips.

The tool falls. Clatters. And then drops into the coolant liquid.

He snatches it before it can sink to the bottom – plunging his hand into the coolant up to the wrist.

As he withdraws his hand, a thin film of ice covers his skin –

– which breaks apart as he balls his fingers into a fist.

INT. MED CENTER

Cassie sits in the Med Center, looking at Trey.

The door to the Med Center opens.

Cassie looks round. It's Capa.

Capa and Cassie talk quietly throughout, as if conscious that, even through his coma, Trey might overhear them.

CAPA

How is he?

Cassie shrugs.

CASSIE

In deeper space than we are.

A beat.

CAPA

It wasn't him that made the mistake, Cassie. It was me.

CASSIE

(*cuts in*)

It was Kaneda. (*Firm.*) Whatever Mace says. Whatever you feel. Or Trey feels. Kaneda was the Captain. He made the mistake.

She turns back to Trey.

And anyway, it's done now.

EXT. ICARUS I

Icarus I floats in space.

Icarus I is the same design as Icarus II, but older, rougher.

In the Sun-shaded section of the vast hull, the shield has been punctured in places by asteroids, through which indirect light reveals something of what is hidden behind the shields . . .

. . . a vast shape implied, but not revealed.

Then, continuing around the ship, revealing . . .

Icarus II, sunlit, closing in on Icarus I at approach speed.

INT. FLIGHT DECK

Mace, Corazon and Harvey watch as Cassie pilots Icarus II towards Icarus I.

INT. OBSERVATION ROOM

Searle and Capa watch the same view from the Observation Room . . .

Capa glances sideways at Searle. The psychiatrist's expression is oddly transfixed by the sight of their stranded forerunner.

SEARLE
(*privately*)

My mistake.

CAPA

. . . What?

SEARLE

The trials for deep space. All that time testing long-term sensory deprivation. Darkness. Emptiness.

Reflected light from their shield illuminates the previously shadowed area of Icarus I. Between that sight and the light beams through the punctured shield, it is arrestingly beautiful.

But actually, our senses aren't deprived at all.

INT. FLIGHT DECK

On the monitors, we see, as the ship comes around, the portal to the Oxygen Garden. It is bright, lit up. Through the portal we can see thick greenery.

CASSIE

Looks like they've still got power.

MACE

Not necessarily. The garden is lit by fibre optics.

CORAZON

The main thing is the plants are still alive. We found our O2.

Mace is checking separate readouts.

MACE

Cassie – are you reading what I'm reading?

CASSIE

She's in orbit.

MACE

It's not deteriorating at all. She could circle like this until the end of time. (*Beat.*) They must have stopped her deliberately.

CORAZON

Repairs?

MACE

Who knows?

Harvey gets down to business.

HARVEY

Okay. So we're basically doing the same manoeuvre as initiating the payload delivery sequence. Then it's just a question of bringing the airlocks together.

CASSIE

Easier said than done, Harvey. These two ships were never meant to dock.

MACE

Just watch the thrust when you decouple the front and back. It's going to push the payload away from us. Fast.

CASSIE

Icarus will handle the reverse boosters.

MACE

I'm saying. Just watch the payload.

CASSIE

I heard you the first time, Mace. Relax.

INT. AIRLOCK

Capa, Mace, Searle and Harvey stand in the airlock.

Searle is wearing his shades, and he is very badly sunburned, his face a patchwork of red and peeling skin.

All crew wear white backpacks. These will be revealed as power-packs.

Silence. Tension.

Broken by Icarus.

ICARUS

Ship-to-ship docking process will commence.

INT/EXT. ICARUS II/FLIGHT DECK

The docking sequence begins, intercut with Cassie in the Flight Deck.

The two ships are positioned so that the shadows from their shields overlap.

Cassie lifts a security case over a section of her console, revealing a switch marked: PAYLOAD SEPARATION.

It has a small keyboard to type in a password.

She types: SUNSHINE.

CASSIE

Firing separation ring. Three, two, one . . .

She turns the switch.

There is a ring of detonations between the rear part of Icarus II and the main body of the ship . . .

. . . and the two sections detach.

As Mace warned, the detonations cause the entire payload section to propel away from the rear section of the ship.

CASSIE
(*quick*)

Icarus?

ICARUS

Yes, Cassie.

Reverse boosters fire, and slow the Payload's trajectory away from the rear section.

CASSIE

Had me worried there.

And we can see it, on her face, a sheen of sweat, as she starts to guide the detached section of the ship toward Icarus I.

The rear section, which contains all the living quarters, is the part of the ship that will perform the dock, within the overlap shadow caused by the two shields.

Outside the ship, we can see the intricacy of the manoeuvre she is performing, as the awkward shape of the rear section drifts towards Icarus I, rotating and stabilizing under brief bursts from the directional jets.

CORAZON

Four hundred metres . . . closing . . .

CASSIE

Rotating to align. Icarus, maintain shield in exact current position relative to Icarus I. Keep us in the shade.

ICARUS

Affirmative, Cassie.

CORAZON

Two hundred metres . . . one-eighty . . . you're speeding up.

CASSIE

I know. I'm on it.

INT. AIRLOCK

CORAZON
(*over comms link*)

One-hundred-fifty metres.

Mace's eyes flick sideways to Searle.

MACE

Nice tan.

Searle ignores this.

Looks great. Healthy.

Harvey cuts in.

HARVEY

Drop it, Mace.

MACE

Drop what? That I'm the only one who seems to notice that our Psych Officer's skin is falling off his bones? That he's half-blind? Okay, I'll drop it.

HARVEY

I'm going in there, he's going in there, and so are you. And that is a direct order.

A moment – in which we can see that Harvey is commander of this vessel in title only.

MACE

Yes, Captain.

INT. FLIGHT DECK

CORAZON

Eighty metres. Seventy. Sixty. It's too fast, Cassie.

CASSIE

Got to get boosters clear of living quarters before firing. Almost there . . .

Outside, the ship is continuing to turn, moving towards a position where the two vessels are at ninety degrees to each other. When they hit ninety degrees –

CASSIE

Clear of living quarters. Firing retro-boosters.

Cassie hits a button.

Outside, we see the retro-boosters fire –

– and the jets strike against protuberances of Icarus I, blowing away particle matter.

CORAZON

You're going to burn a hole in their storage capsules.

CASSIE

They'll hold.

CORAZON

Still closing too fast! Check alignment!

CASSIE

Alignment good. Trajectory good.

CORAZON

Thirty metres! Twenty!

CASSIE

(*calm*)

Brace for impact. Might scratch the paintwork.

EXT. ICARUS II

We watch as the rear section of Icarus II closes in on Icarus I. It is visibly too fast.

The docking lights align, showing the male to female ports.

Then, with a sickening thump, the two airlocks meet.

INT. FLIGHT DECK

The sound of the connection, the scraping metal and the juddering impact, resound through the ship.

Then silence.

CASSIE

Okay. (*Beat.*) We're locked on.

Only now does Cassie realize she is bathed in sweat. But her voice does not betray the relief at having successfully docked.

A handkerchief flops in front of her.

Tossed by Corazon.

Cassie takes it, shooting a smile at Corazon, and wipes her face.

Icarus, please establish contact with Icarus I computer system.

ICARUS

Contact failed. Computer system of Icarus I is non-functioning. Reasons unknown. Impossible to establish the cause remotely.

CORAZON

Atmosphere?

ICARUS

Oxygen-rich. Fully breathable and life-supporting.

A beat.

CASSIE

And is it supporting any life?

ICARUS

Unknown.

Silence.

CASSIE

Guys. Did you get all that?

HARVEY

(*over radio link*)

We got it.

CASSIE

So you heard her. It's breathable. In your own time, you're good to go. (*Beat.*) Be careful in there.

INT. ICARUS I/AIRLOCK

Inside the airlock of Icarus I.

The design of the interior of Icarus I is similar to Icarus II, but feels slightly more dated, clearly an earlier model.

The airlock is dark, half-lit . . .

. . . until the airlock opens, revealing the bright interior of the Icarus II airlock, and the four men about to board.

Each carries a flashlights, and . . .

INT. FLIGHT DECK

. . . head-cams, which are watched by Cassie and Corazon on the Flight Deck monitor.

INT. ICARUS I/AIRLOCK

The four sweep their flashlight beams around the dark airlock.

In the beams, the atmosphere is surprisingly thick with motes of dust.

HARVEY

Cassie – are you getting this on the feed?

CASSIE

(*over comms link*)

Getting what?

HARVEY

The air is full of . . . dust.

SEARLE

Human skin.

HARVEY

What?

SEARLE

Eighty percent of dust is human skin.

Beat.

Mace has found a control panel, which he uses . . .

And nothing happens.

HARVEY

No lights.

SEARLE

No surprise.

Mace opens the door to the airlock manually, and aims his flashlight into the pitch-black corridor beyond.

MACE

Anyone afraid of the dark?

Silence.

MACE

We should split up.

HARVEY

I'm not sure that's a good idea.

MACE

(dry)

Maybe you're right. If we split up, we might get picked off one at a time by aliens.

SEARLE

(to Harvey)

Icarus I is a big ship. We can't search it effectively if we're in a single group.

HARVEY

Okay, okay. Mace, head for the Flight Deck. See if she can fly, and get these lights working again. Searle, check the social area and the sleeping quarters. Capa, aim for the payload. And I'll check the Oxygen Garden.

INT. ICARUS I/SOCIAL AREA – PITCH BLACK

A flashlight picks up a dust-covered framed picture.

A hand wipes the dust away, revealing a freeze-frame of the crew of Icarus I.

We've seen this before. But the crew of Icarus I are dressed in superhero outfits, and the glass of the frame has been broken.

Next, the flashlight passes across an open compartment in the kitchen area. It is full of food.

Next, Searle presses the button on the water dispenser – and a steady stream spills out from the tap.

SEARLE

Water. Food supplies. Oxygen. (*Beat.*) But no crew. No bodies.

Searle illuminates something else.

Gouged into the social area table are some graffiti . . .

. . . depicting the solar system.

A mini-basketball is the Sun. Ball-bearings make the planets.

Close to the Sun is an 'X' mark, and three scratched words: YOU ARE HERE.

SEARLE

It's a ghost ship.

INT. ICARUS I/AIRLOCK TO PAYLOAD BAY – PITCH BLACK

Capa is moving through the airlock between the living quarters and the payload bay.

As the airlock opens, there is a rush of pressurized air, which kicks up the dust around him.

INT. ICARUS I/FLIGHT DECK – PITCH BLACK

Mace pulls open the door to the Flight Deck . . .

. . . to reveal stillness. Quiet. Every monitor showing a black and lifeless screen.

INT. ICARUS I/OXYGEN GARDEN

Harvey is in the glass corridor that leads into the Oxygen Garden.

Unlike the rest of the ship, this area is bright.

The sides of the corridor are crowded with thick foliage.

HARVEY

Seven years of unchecked growth. The ecosystem is working beautifully. You ought to see this, Cory.

INT. FLIGHT DECK

Cassie and Corazon are watching Harvey's live feed.

CORAZON

It's wonderful.

INT. ICARUS I/FLIGHT DECK – PITCH BLACK

Mace is at the engineer's station, in front of a monitor screen.

We now learn the function of the white backpacks – as Mace reaches behind him and pulls out a flex, which he inserts into a female socket on the console.

Immediately, the console screen lights up with static.

Mace starts working switches.

The fuzz leaves the monitor, and is replaced by data streams.

MACE

Strange.

The other monitors all start to flicker back into life.

MACE

Sub-systems are fine. Solar harvest is fine. The ship should be up and running, except . . . I'm getting nothing from the flight computer. I think the mainframe is down.

He works some more switches, then –

– on the monitor in front of him, a frozen image appears on the screen.

A man.

The man's head is bowed. Hidden from us.

It is Pinbacker.

MACE

(*under his breath*)

. . . Shit. (*Into comms link.*) Guys. I just found one of the ghosts.

He pushes a button. The image unfreezes, and starts to play.

Pinbacker starts to speak. His voice is tired, broken. Despairing. This is a final message, recorded on a dying ship.

PINBACKER

My name is Captain Pinbacker.

INT. FLIGHT DECK

Cassie and Corazon watch the recording on Mace's head-cam.

PINBACKER
(*voice-over*)
My ship's mission was to keep the sun shining. But the mission has failed.

INT. ICARUS I/OXYGEN GARDEN

Harvey stands in the Icarus I Oxygen Garden.

PINBACKER
(*voice-over*)
There may be time and materials for Earth to construct and send a second mission. But that mission will fail too. It will fail for the same reason as ours.

The foliage has run riot.

INT. ICARUS I/SLEEPING QUARTERS – PITCH BLACK

Searle is looking into one of the partitions of the sleeping quarters.

Inside, the space has been customized by the crew members. There are photos stuck to the wall, and lying on the bed, face down, is a paperback book – written in Chinese.

Searle picks it up. After lying for seven years in a face-down position, the spine holds its shape perfectly.

PINBACKER
(*voice-over*)
I'm now recording a final message. I'll broadcast it into the solar winds, and the words will be lost in the flares of a dying star.

INT. ICARUS I/STELLAR BOMB – PITCH BLACK

Capa is standing on the gantry inside the bomb.

PINBACKER
(*voice-over*)
And when I die, I'll be the message.

Ahead, the console is picked up by his flashlight.

Delivered to the face of God.

INT. ICARUS I/COMMS CENTER – PITCH BLACK

Back on Pinbacker . . .

As his head raises. Revealing his face.

Which is sunburned.

Pinbacker smiles.

Then the image freezes, then distorts, then is replaced by the words: TRANSMISSION ENDS – 13.10.79.

A long beat.

MACE

Okay . . . That make sense to anyone?

INT. ICARUS I/CORRIDOR – PITCH BLACK

Searle is standing in a corridor.

Looking at something strange.

On the wall in front of Searle is what looks like a shadow. The silhouette of a man, like the burned imprints on the walls of Hiroshima.

The man has one arm raised, as if he was shielding his eyes at the moment he was imprinted.

Searle lifts a finger towards the burned silhouette, and wipes a finger across it.

The tip of his finger comes away black.

On the wall behind him, opposite the shadow mark, is a closed door. On the door, it reads: OBSERVATION ROOM.

INT. FLIGHT DECK

CORAZON

His last message home?

MACE

(*over comms link*)

The transmission code is six and a half years ago.

CORAZON

That would be after they entered non-com zone. In fact, it would be around the time they were supposed to deliver the payload.

CASSIE

(*quiet, to herself*)

What happened in there?

CORAZON

Whatever it was, doesn't feel like an accident.

INT. ICARUS I/STELLAR BOMB – PITCH BLACK

Capa works the console.

His power pack is plugged in.

Data streams pour across the screen.

Then he interrupts them by touching a button on the console – marked TEST SEQUENCE.

As he does so, he turns.

Looks up into the void of the bomb.

Waiting for something. Scanning the darkness.

Then –

– popping out of nowhere, taking Capa slightly by surprise . . .

. . . a single spark appears.

Glowing. Fizzing. Dancing in the darkness like a firefly.

Capa watches it a few moments.

Then he turns, hits a button on the console –

– and the spark vanishes.

Capa nods. Smiles.

CAPA

The payload is operational.

CASSIE

(*over comms link*)

Say again, Capa?

CAPA

The payload is fully operational. It's A-okay.

INT. ICARUS I/ICARUS MAINFRAME – PITCH BLACK

On Mace's face as he enters a new area.

From the Icarus II flight deck, the sound of Corazon cheering comes through over the comms link.

CASSIE

(*over comms link*)

That's great news, Capa. Congratulations. Looks like we've got what we came for.

But Mace isn't cheering with them. His face is a mask.

MACE

(*cuts in*)

No we haven't.

We can see now that Mace has entered the compartment that houses the Icarus mainframe.

Sudden silence over the comms.

CASSIE

(*over comms link*)

. . . Go ahead, Mace.

MACE

I've found the reason for the distress signal. The black box beacon was triggered automatically in the event of terminal malfunction of the Icarus mainframe . . .

The glass panels, embedded with their beautifully intricate circuitry, have been raised out of the coolant liquid . . .

. . . and they are badly damaged. As if by fire.

. . . And believe me, this is terminal. There's been a coolant failure of some kind. Bottom line: it doesn't matter that Capa's payload is operational. Without the Icarus system we can't fly.

Silence.

We shouldn't be here. We should never have gone off mission.

INT. FLIGHT DECK

Cassie and Corazon exchange a glance.

As behind them . . .

. . . Trey appears. Haggard, silent, unnoticed.

He has the quality of an apparition.

Then he is gone.

INT. ICARUS I/STELLAR BOMB – PITCH BLACK

Capa's face.

Recalling Kaneda's death.

Then:

SEARLE

(*over comms link*)

I have something to say. (*Beat.*) I've found the crew.

INT. ICARUS I/OBSERVATION ROOM

An extraordinary sight.

Through the Observation Room window, we can see the shield of Icarus II, protecting the room from the glare of the Sun.

In the Observation Room, amidst dancing dust motes, are seven figures.

Some are seated, or slumped. Two are lying on the ground.

One is actually standing.

They are all blackened, burned in a flash that allowed them to maintain their form, like carbon statues.

In fact, very like statues. One, like the Venus de Milo, has its arms missing below the elbows. Another, like the Sphinx, has lost its nose.

Another has lost two fingers.

Another has lost the left side of its head, as if half the skull has slewed away like a landslide.

Amongst them, Searle and Capa stand.

CAPA

. . . What happened?

SEARLE

They had an epiphany. They saw the light.

A beat – it is unclear if Searle is joking.

In response to Capa's gaze:

I suspect that the observation filter is fully open. If we weren't behind the shield of Icarus II, we'd join them.

Searle reaches out and touches one of the bodies on the side of the arm.

Under his touch, like a desiccated sand-sculpture, the arm breaks and falls away. Turning to dust.

The dust that fills the ship.

SEARLE

Ashes to ashes, stardust to stardust.

MACE

No shit.

Capa and Searle turn to see Mace. Who has joined them.

MACE

(*into his comms link*)

Cassie – whatever you do, don't let the shield move until we're . . .

At that moment –

– a sudden wrenching sound. Loud and freakish, like tearing metal.

Mace breaks off.

What the hell was that?

And the next moment – the entire ship gives a sudden lurch.

Harvey is knocked off balance, and is sent crashing sideways into the wall and down to the floor . . .

. . . as the carbonized bodies of the Icarus I crew vaporize.

INT. FLIGHT DECK

Icarus II is lurching too.

Cassie is hitting buttons on the console, flicking switches.

Over the radio link we can hear the shouts of alarm of Capa, Mace, Harvey and Searle.

CORAZON

Icarus! Stabilize us!

ICARUS

Affirmative, Corazon.

CAPA

(*over radio link*)

What is it? What's happening?

CASSIE

Capa! Get to the airlock *now*!

INT. ICARUS I – PITCH BLACK

We follow Capa, Mace and Searle as they run through Icarus I to the airlock.

And when they reach it . . .

INT. ICARUS I/OXYGEN GARDEN/CORRIDOR

Harvey runs from the Oxygen Garden into the corridor.

INT. ICARUS I/OUTSIDE AIRLOCK – PITCH BLACK

Capa moves past Searle, and presses his face to the glass of the outer airlock.

He can see that the airlock door is open to outer space.

And he can see the airlock door of Icarus I, which is also open, and the reason for the sound of tearing metal we heard.

Around the door of Icarus I the skin of the ship has been ripped open, revealing the hull structure beneath.

Icarus II floats twenty or thirty metres away.

And around the ripped airlock of Icarus I, we can see, in several places, gases are venting from the ship.

Oxygen.

MACE

Cassie?

INT. FLIGHT DECK

CASSIE

The airlock has decoupled. We don't know why. The locking system on Icarus I is totally ripped open. I can hold our current position, but we aren't going to be able to dock again. (*Beat.*) But there's something else, guys. You've got a hull breach. I can see it. You're losing atmosphere.

INT. ICARUS I/OUTSIDE AIRLOCK – PITCH BLACK

CAPA

We're screwed.

Mace – thinking fast.

MACE

No.

He goes to the sub-compartment holding the mirrored space suits.

Of the three suits, only one remains.

One of us isn't, at any rate.

EXT. ICARUS I

The outside of the ship, venting gas.

INT. ICARUS I/OUTSIDE AIRLOCK – PITCH BLACK

Harvey arrives –

– to find Capa suited up, minus helmet.

HARVEY

What's happened?

MACE

The airlock is destroyed. There's only one suit. Capa's taking it.

Silence.

HARVEY

. . . Why Capa?

MACE

Because the rest of us are a lower priority.

Harvey is thinking fast. But not clearly.

HARVEY

I'm not a low priority.

MACE

You're a Comms Officer, on a ship without any means of communication.

HARVEY

I'm the *Captain*! The mission needs a Captain *to hold it together*!

SEARLE

Capa is the only person outside Icarus who can operate the payload. There's no choice.

HARVEY

There's no choice for *you*. (*Turns to Capa.*) Capa, as Captain, I order you to remove that suit.

Capa does not respond in any way.

That is a direct order. You can rest assured that once I am on board Icarus II, I will do everything in my power to –

MACE

– to what? Shuttle back? With more suits? (*He jabs a hand at the inner airlock door.*) The airlock is ripped in half, Harvey. Once that seal is broken, how do we repressurize?

Beat.

(*Into radio link.*) Cassie, I've got a plan here.

CASSIE

Go.

MACE

We can't depressurize when we open the airlock for Capa. So the force of the expelled gas is going to fire him out, right?

CASSIE

(*over radio link*)

Right.

MACE

Okay. If you have your airlock open, and you line it up right, he'll fire right inside. (*Beat.*) And so will we.

INT. FLIGHT DECK

Cassie and Corazon exchange a glance.

CORAZON

Without suits?

MACE

(*over radio link*)

Get as close as you can.

CASSIE

You'll have twenty metres to cover.

CORAZON

. . . At minus two hundred and seventy-three degrees Celsius.

MACE

(*over radio link*)

It's going to be cold, but we'll make it.

Silence.

Anyone got any better ideas?

Silence.

Copy that.

INT. ICARUS I/AIRLOCK – PITCH BLACK

Mace and Harvey are stripping the inner airlock for padding, materials, anything they can use to swaddle themselves.

But Searle is not.

SEARLE

(*calm*)

Mace. One problem. The computer is down, one of us is going to have to manually operate the seal . . .

Mace breaks off.

MACE

(*finishes*)

. . . from the inside. (*He closes his eyes.*) Shit. (*Then meets Searle's gaze.*) You're right.

SEARLE

So whatever happens, someone is staying behind.

Silence. An understanding between Searle and Mace.

Which Harvey misreads.

HARVEY

(*shaking*)

I see. I get it. So it's me, right? That's what you're all thinking.

SEARLE

No, Harvey. It's me.

INT. CAPA'S HELMET

Inside Capa's helmet as it is placed over his head by Searle.

Time is short.

We can only hear the sound of Capa breathing.

With the locking mechanism in place, Searle looks directly into Capa's helmet.

He says something to Capa.

SEARLE

We're only stardust.

But Capa can't hear him. He can only see the movement of his lips.

CAPA

I can't hear you.

Inside the helmet, Capa's words sound unnaturally loud.

INT. ICARUS I/OUTSIDE AIRLOCK – PITCH BLACK

Searle is gone.

Mace and Capa and Harvey wait.

MACE

Okay. We've got just one shot at this. You ready, Cassie?

CASSIE

(*over radio link*)

I'm ready.

MACE

Okay.

Mace and Harvey approach Capa, and lock their arms tight around him.

Let's do it.

From outside, Searle opens the door to the airlock.

Immediately, all three men are sucked out into the airlock . . .

. . . then ejected through the broken outer door, and into outer space.

INT. ICARUS I/AIRLOCK – PITCH BLACK

The three men shoot through the airlock, propelled by the evacuating gases.

As they pass through the broken area, Harvey's shoulder catches twisted metal.

His shoulder visibly breaks, and he is wounded with a deep gash.

Blood sprays out –

– and freezes immediately.

EXT. ICARUS II

Silence as . . .

. . . we watch Mace, Capa and Harvey shoot out from Icarus I, towards Icarus II . . .

. . . in the weightlessness of space, they have no control over themselves.

They fire across the short distance between Icarus I and II . . .

. . . then collide hard against the side of the Icarus II.

The impact is shocking.

Mace bounces off, away from the airlock.

But he is caught by Capa.

But Harvey is not.

He has struck the hull at an odd angle, and is now falling down the side of Icarus II.

A strange, slow sequence.

Harvey is only a couple of metres from the side of the ship.

When he reaches out his hand, his fingertips are only an inch from the side of the hull.

But he is in zero-gravity vacuum. There is nothing he can do to affect his trajectory.

He twists. Stretches. Strains.

All to no effect.

And now we can see that he is literally freezing as he falls.

His eyes open and ice over at once.

He opens his mouth to scream . . .

. . . and as he does so, the moisture in his breath crystallizes – hanging in a sparkling dust-cloud around his mouth.

In this posture, he dies.

But we stay with him.

Down the length of the ship, until his hand strikes a protuberance –

– and his frozen arm smashes off –

– and his corpse spins off into space . . .

. . . until it is unshielded from the sunlight.

INT. AIRLOCK

The airlock is repressurized.

Mace is collapsed on the floor.

Corazon and Cassie rush in to help Mace.

Capa leans back against the airlock wall.

He reaches up and releases the locks to his helmet, and removes it.

CAPA
(*quiet*)

Jesus.

Fade to:

EXT. ICARUS II

Icarus II fires its booster.

EXT. ICARUS I

From the position of Icarus I, we watch Icarus II power away.

As it does so, the Observation Room of Icarus I becomes unshielded from the Sun's glare.

INT. ICARUS I/OBSERVATION ROOM

Searle stands in the Oxygen Garden, watching Icarus II depart.

INT. ICARUS I/OUTSIDE OBSERVATION ROOM

Searle is outside the Observation Room door. And the shadow of the man, shielding his eyes.

Searle opens the door, and as soon as he does so –

– an incredibly fierce light breaks out.

The light is so bright and intense that it looks almost like solid mass. A block of photons.

It blazes over the shadow on the opposite wall.

A moment. Then Searle reveals what he has been holding in his hands.

His sunglasses.

He puts them on, and steps into the light.

EXT. ICARUS I/OBSERVATION ROOM

Pure light.

And in it . . .

. . . we watch as Searle is carbonized, then bleached away to nothingness.

Fade to:

INT. SOCIAL AREA

The monitor shows Trey lying in the Med Center.

Capa, Mace, Corazon and Cassie are at the table. The remaining empty seats say everything they need to.

MACE

I've been through Icarus's activity log and it checked out. Then I double-checked, and Cory tripled – same result. In other words, unless Icarus is deleting her own files, it wasn't her.

CORAZON

And there's no malfunction on the airlock hardware.

MACE

Which means the airlock was manually decoupled.

A moment of silence, taking in the implication.

CORAZON

Cassie and I were together on the Flight Deck the whole time.

MACE

As were Capa and Searle. We can all assume it wasn't Harvey. And I know it wasn't me, even if you guys don't. So the way I see it, that only leaves one possibility.

Mace breaks off. Takes a deep breath. This is hard for him.

MACE

Trey.

CAPA

Trey is so doped up he can hardly walk or feed himself. He sleeps twenty-three hours a day. And he blames himself for everything that has gone wrong. Why would he do it?

MACE

We don't know. But the possibility remains that it was him. And we have to take that seriously.

CAPA

By doping him up more?

Mace and Corazon exchange a glance.

CORAZON

This isn't just about the possibility he sabotaged the airlock. There's something else too. When Searle and Harvey died, we lost two breathers. (*Beat.*) If Trey dies, we'll have the oxygen to make it to the delivery point.

This is what Mace and Corazon were building to, and the logic is truly powerful. Undeniable.

CASSIE

(*flat*)

You're saying we kill him.

CAPA

At least we now know what happened on Icarus I: the same thing that's happening here.

MACE

What are you trying to remind me of, Capa? My lost humanity? Give me a fucking break. (*Beat.*) I'll be the one to do it. I'm not passing any bucks.

CASSIE

Do it how?

MACE

That's between me and Trey.

A moment.

This time, we vote. Unanimous decision required. (*Beat.*) So. You know where I stand.

CORAZON

And me.

A beat.

Mace and Corazon wait.

CAPA

What are you asking? We weigh the life of one against the future of mankind? (*Beat.*) Kill him.

Mace nods.

CORAZON

Cassie?

All look to her.

She looks a thousand miles away. A hundred thousand.

CASSIE

No.

Silence.

MACE

Cassie –

CASSIE

(cuts in)

I know the arguments. I know the logic. (*Beat.*) You say you need my vote. And I'm saying you can't have it.

Silence.

CORAZON

So what do we do?

Silence.

Then Mace stands.

Cassie closes her eyes.

CASSIE

Oh God.

MACE

I'm sorry, Cassie.

CASSIE

(tears roll down her face)

Make it easy for him. Somehow. Find a kindness.

INT. ICARUS II

We follow Mace as he walks through Icarus II to the Med Center.

INT. MED CENTER

Mace enters the Med Center.

He walks over to a compartment, which he opens, revealing surgical knives and equipment.

Note: on the tray, two of the blades are already missing.

A moment, as Mace chooses a knife.

He checks the balance and grip in his hand, then turns and sees . . .

. . . for the first time, that Trey is not there.

The bed is empty.

A moment.

Then, at the entrance to the Earth Room, he sees a smear of blood.

Mace goes to the entrance to the Earth Room.

Looks inside.

A beat.

Then he speaks into his comms link.

MACE

Everyone. Get here now.

INT. MED CENTER/EARTH ROOM

Mace enters.

Blue sky. Clouds moving.

Then, over the clouds, a frozen spray of blood.

We reveal Trey.

Dead.

Mace crouches beside Trey. Holds his hand.

Capa, Cassie and Corazon appear.

Corazon kneels beside Trey and picks up a Med Center scalpel.

CORAZON

He cut his wrists.

MACE

(*quiet*)

Looks like he beat me to it.

A moment. Then:

All these deaths: Kaneda, Harvey, Searle, Trey. None of them would have happened . . . (*Looks to Capa.*) . . . if you hadn't diverted the mission.

CAPA

What do you want me to say?

MACE

You don't have to say shit. I just want you to know.

Mace stands and approaches Capa. His hand is smeared with Trey's blood.

That this . . .

He grabs Capa's wrist, and smears Trey's blood onto Capa's hands.

. . . Belongs here.

A moment.

Then a flash of movement – as Capa attacks Mace.

The two go flying out into the Med Center.

Corazon hardly responds.

INT. MED CENTER

The two men struggle, but the fight is quickly losing its steam – for both men.

Both break and slide to the floor, gasping for air.

Mace shakes his head, dazed.

MACE

You son of a bitch.

He starts to get up, but almost as if he's drunk, doesn't make it halfway, and slides back down.

Silence.

In which, we notice, both are breathing in the same slightly laboured way. Their breaths slightly deeper than they should be.

They notice at the same moment that we do.

At that moment –

– Cassie passes. Without looking at them.

CORAZON

Air's low. We need to start limiting our exertions.

She leaves.

Mace and Capa continue listening to each other's breathing.

EXT. THE SUN

The Sun dominates the view.

Icarus II is dwarfed by it. A speck, against the raging fire.

INT. OBSERVATION ROOM

The Sun blazes large in the Observation Room.

Passing between many filters.

Multicolored.

Then –

– we see there is someone silhouetted on the seat.

We can't make out which of the crew it is. The light is disguising their precise shape, making them seem slimmer than they could be. Arms and neck too thin. Head an ellipse. Almost alien.

INT. CORRIDOR

Mace sits in a corridor.

INT. OXYGEN GARDEN

Corazon sits in the Oxygen Garden.

INT. CASSIE'S BUNK

Cassie lies in her bunk. She is weeping.

A shadow passes outside her bunk.

INT. ICARUS MAINFRAME

Synapse sparks flare up across the circuit boards . . .

. . . and the temperature on the digital readout starts to creep up.

INT. STELLAR BOMB

Capa stands on the gantry, in front of the console. As we have seen him before, he is watching fluid streams of data pass across the monitor screen.

ICARUS

Capa.

CAPA

Yes.

ICARUS

Warning. The biometric data on your comms link is showing that your oxygen consumption is insufficient.

Capa looks down – and sees that the small blinking light on his comms link has begun to pulse red instead of blue.

CAPA

Thank you, Icarus.

Silence. Then:

ICARUS

Capa.

CAPA

Yes.

ICARUS

You are dying. All crew are dying.

CAPA

We know we're dying. As long as we live long enough to deliver the payload, we're okay with it.

Silence. Then:

ICARUS

Capa. Warning.

Beat.

You will not live long enough to deliver the payload.

For the first time, Capa looks up from the console, away from the data streams.

CAPA

Please clarify.

ICARUS

Two hours, before crew will be unable to perform complex tasks. Four hours, before crew will be unable to perform basic tasks. Six hours until death. Journey time to delivery point: nine hours.

CAPA

That's impossible. Corazon was certain: we have remaining oxygen to keep *four* crew alive.

ICARUS

Affirmative. Four crew could potentially survive on current reserves.

CAPA

. . . But Trey's dead. There *are* only four crew members.

ICARUS

Negative.

CAPA

Affirmative, Icarus. Four crew. Mace, Cassie, Corazon and me.

ICARUS

Five crew members.

Capa's face. Sudden cold realization. Dawning.

CAPA

Icarus.

ICARUS

Yes, Capa.

CAPA

Who is the fifth crew member?

ICARUS

Unknown.

A long beat.

CAPA

. . . Where is the fifth crew member?

ICARUS

In the Observation Room.

INT. OBSERVATION ROOM

Capa opens the door to the Observation Room . . .

. . . and is bathed in light.

The Sun is huge. Taking up all of the portal.

For a few moments, Capa watches the solar flares explode outwards from the boiling surface.

Then, resolving through the image, we see that there is a figure, standing in front of the portal.

Dwarfed by it. Enveloped by the Sun.

Then the figure turns.

A strange effect – the Man, who is naked, is so fiercely backlit that his skin is translucent. We can see his bones, his organs, the shadow of his skull.

A moment, as Capa and the Man face each other.

Then the Man speaks.

MAN

Are you an angel?

Capa seems too stunned to even reply.

Has the moment come? I've been waiting. So long.

CAPA

. . . Who are you?

MAN

Who am I?

Beat.

At the end of time, a moment will come in which just one man remains. Then the moment will pass. The man will be gone. There will be nothing left to know that we were ever here, but stardust.

Beat.

Am I that man?

Now on Capa's face – as he realizes, suddenly, who he is talking to.

CAPA

My God. Pinbacker.

Behind Pinbacker now, a colossal solar flare reaches out from the Sun as if to claim him.

PINBACKER

Not your God. *Mine.*

Capa frowns.

Then looks down.

On the material of his shirt, behind a long slice in the fabric, a blossoming flower of blood is spreading around his stomach.

Dazed, he takes a step backwards.

He looks back up at Pinbacker.

As he does so, we see his comms unit fall from around his neck – the cord cut.

And now we see, in Pinbacker's hand – the knife he used to kill Trey.

Pinbacker raises the knife, about to slice Capa's neck.

CAPA
(*yells*)

Icarus! Full sunlight!

Sunlight fills the room – bleaching everything to whiteness.

INT. CORRIDOR/OUTSIDE OBSERVATION ROOM

The corridor outside the Observation Room.

The door to the Observation Room opens, and light floods out.

On his hands and knees, Capa scrambles out.

His stomach area is wet with blood.

He tries to get up.

He trips – falls sideways.

He's blinking, tears streaming from his eyes, temporarily half-blinded.

He picks himself up, and stumbling, arms outstretched, starts to run.

He runs out of shot.

Moments later . . .

Pinbacker steps out of the Observation Room.

He stands a moment in the blaze – upright, backlit by the sunlight from the open Observation Room.

A blackened silhouette shape.

The door behind him closes.

And now we can see that where the sunlight had been blazing against his naked back, the skin is not steaming but smoking.

Even burning. Tiny flames lick on the edges of crusts of skin, that glow like coal embers, or miniature lava streams.

Unconcerned by what must be immeasurable pain, Pinbacker turns in the direction Capa fled, and gives chase.

INT. CORRIDOR TO OXYGEN GARDEN

Capa is running along the long corridor that links the living quarters to the back of the ship.

He tries to call out. To call for Icarus or Mace. But he's too short of breath.

Capa looks behind him – and sees Pinbacker's black, smoking figure running after him, at the far end of the corridor.

Gasping, Capa runs again.

INT. CORRIDOR INTERSECTION

Pinbacker chases Capa through the intersection.

INT. AIRLOCK

Capa has run into the airlock.

A total dead end.

Panic on Capa's face.

Capa turns and sees Pinbacker entering the airlock.

Capa lunges for a panel, and a handle –

– and the glass interior pressure door slides shut, sealing Capa in the airlock, and Pinbacker on the other side.

Pinbacker stops at the door.

Checks it.

Tries to open it.

Then sees the handle that Capa just pulled. Above it, it simply reads: MANUAL LOCK.

A moment, as Pinbacker and Capa face each other through the glass . . .

. . . and we see the Pinbacker's face clearly for the first time since we saw him on the broadcast.

Pinbacker's skin is so sun-damaged and eaten with melanomas we can hardly recognize him.

The moment is held.

Then:

Pinbacker lifts his hand and presses the panel on his *side of the door.*

Then:

Pinbacker turns, and leaves.

A silent beat.

Capa peers through the glass.

Pinbacker definitely seems to have gone.

The first thing Capa does is to lift his shirt and check his wound.

Across his stomach is a deep slash. Blood is welling out fast.

CAPA

Oh Christ.

Capa checks again for Pinbacker through the glass. Then, with fingers slick with blood, he presses the panel on his side of the door.

And nothing happens.

Capa peers through the glass and sees that on the reverse side of the airlock, Pinbacker has done exactly the same thing he did. The panel door is open, and the handle marked manual lock is pulled down.

Pinbacker has locked Capa in.

A beat.

Capa slams his fist against the glass.

Cut to reverse side of glass, where Capa rages and punches the glass in total silence.

INT. OXYGEN GARDEN – WORK LIGHTS

Corazon is sitting in the ashes of the Oxygen Garden, which is still lit by the work-lights she erected.

Gazing into middle distance.

Then focusing . . .

. . . on something.

Frowning, she gets up, then walks towards the area that held the larger plants, at the bottom of the sloping roof, where condensation ran down to form a pool.

She kneels there. Her eyes widen.

CORAZON

. . . You're kidding me.

She looks closer. And we see what she sees. Under the ashes, just poking through, a tiny flash of emerald.

She blows gently at the ashes.

And uncovers . . .

. . . a single green shoot.

A tendril, with two small leaves poking out the end.

Corazon gasps.

CORAZON

Oh my God!

For a moment, she almost wells up.

CORAZON

A *baby*. Oh you're beautiful. Too beautiful. (*Laughing.*) Icarus. Patch me through to Mace.

No response.

Icarus. Patch me through to Mace! I've got something *wonderful* to show him.

No response.

Or Cassie. Or Capa.

She breaks off.

Icarus?

Then her eyebrows rise in sudden surprise. Or alarm.

And she sits up, and reaches behind her.

Where we pull back to reveal Pinbacker is holding his knife in her back.

A strange moment.

Corazon is kneeling, trying to reach the knife. Unable to get a hand to it.

Her movements are vague. As if distracted. She is losing focus, before losing consciousness.

Pinbacker is behind her, holding the knife fast.

PINBACKER

Don't fight it. It's not in your destiny to survive. It's not even in your nature. Nothing survives. Not your parents, not your children. Not the birds, or the fishes, or the trees. Not even stars.

Corazon's movements weaken.

She falls backwards, into Pinbacker's arms.

He holds her as she dies. Blinking, mouth opening and closing, then filling with blood.

Then he lets her roll to the side.

Close-up on Pinbacker's face.

In profile, as he leans down over the shoot, putting his lips close to the green . . .

. . . and breathes in, almost kissing the tiny leaves.

INT. ICARUS II

Icarus II hangs in locked orbit.

INT. AIRLOCK

Capa looks around.

Through the glass of the inner airlock door, he sees something.

Past the inner airlock, the lights at the far end of the corridor that leads to the rest of the ship . . .

. . . switch off.

A beat – then the next-nearest set of lights switches off.

It is as if darkness is encroaching on his position.

Capa watches horrified as the darkness gets closer and closer, as the lighting system shuts down . . .

. . . until he is left in a single bubble of light in the outer airlock.

CAPA
(*quiet*)

Oh shit.

Click.

And the lights go out.

INT. CASSIE'S BUNK – DARKNESS

Darkness.

In the darkness, we can make out Cassie, in her bunk.

The soft pulse-glow of her comms link stops.

Her head is cocked to the side, as if listening.

CASSIE

(*into comms link*)

Hey – Capa. Can you hear me?

A silent beat.

All we can hear is Cassie's own breathing.

CASSIE

(*into comms link*)

Mace? Cory? (*Beat.*) Anyone?

INT. SLEEPING QUARTERS – DARKNESS

Cassie opens the partition. She has a flashlight in her hand.

She looks left.

The sleeping quarters seem empty.

She looks right, towards the social area.

And jolts –

A figure is standing at the far end of the sleeping quarters, in the doorway of the social area.

Pinbacker.

Cassie catches her breath at the surreal and demonic shape. In the darkness he is a particularly strange sight. He glows, irradiated, as if lit from inside.

He is not looking in Cassie's direction.

A beat later, Pinbacker's head turns towards her.

Cut to –

INT. CORRIDOR – DARKNESS

Pinbacker's point of view in the Social Area . . .

. . . and Cassie has gone.

INT. ICARUS II – DARKNESS

Mace is walking fast through the ship, picking up equipment as he goes. A flashlight, and battery pack.

MACE

Icarus, please respond.

No response.

Mace taps at his radio link.

(*Into radio link.*) Is anyone else getting silence from Icarus?

No response.

INT. FLIGHT DECK – DARKNESS

Mace enters the Flight Deck.

It is empty.

He shines his flashlight over the monitors. It is a precise echo of the moment he entered the Flight Deck of Icarus I. As before, the monitors are dead.

MACE

(*under his breath*)

What the –?

He goes over to the console, starts working on it. The monitors come on, and the graphics and data flick across the screens.

Emergency lighting comes on.

Icarus! Why are the lights dead? Why are the engines dead? What are we doing in orbit? Respond! *Now!*

As he's talking, he moves to his engineer's station.

He starts flicking through CCTV images of the ship's interior. Images with diagnostics are captioned on the screen:

ENGINE COMPARTMENT ONE: OFFLINE.

ENGINE COMPARTMENT TWO: OFFLINE.

As he scrolls through different images –

– he sees a figure pass across a screen in the darkness.

It's Pinbacker.

MACE

What?

Mace frowns, unsure if he saw what he thought he saw, trying to spot the figure again. Flicking fast through the views. But instead he finds –

Jesus Christ.

– an image on the monitor, captioned: AIRLOCK.

And it shows Capa, hammering on the locked door.

MACE
(*into radio link*)

Capa?

Capa shows no sign of hearing.

Mace reaches to the console and tunes the comms link to the space suits (previously used/established by Cassie to communicate with the crew during the space walk and exploration of Icarus I).

MACE

Capa!

INT. AIRLOCK – EMERGENCY LIGHTING

Capa's head turns to the racked space suit.

He goes over and pulls the comms link out of the helmet, and fits it into his ear.

CAPA

Mace! I copy!

MACE
(*over comms link*)
What the hell is going on? We're in orbit and I can't talk to Icarus and – *shit*!

Mace abruptly cuts off.

CAPA

Mace?

INT. FLIGHT DECK – EMERGENCY LIGHTING

Mace's chair is empty, and on the engineer's monitor screen, a message is flashing on and off.

It reads:

ICARUS MAINFRAME: COOLANT FAILURE.

INT. ICARUS MAINFRAME – EMERGENCY LIGHTING

Close up on Mace's face. He is breathing, steam is rolling from his mouth.

Wherever he is, it's extremely cold.

Pull back to reveal Mace in the Icarus II mainframe . . .

CAPA
(*over comms link*)
Mace – what's going on?

MACE
(*ignoring Capa*)
Oh no . . .

. . . and he is staring in horror at the circuit boards. Not only are these raised out of the coolant tank, but the synapse flares along the circuit pathways have lost their fluidity. They are erratic. Intermittent. Failing.

INT. MED CENTER/EARTH ROOM – DARKNESS

Cassie slips into the Earth Room.

She's holding a long scalpel blade.

The Earth Room images are not functioning, and in the low emergency lighting we see Trey's corpse.

Cassie presses herself against the far wall.

Just Cassie's breathing. Laboured. But trying to keep it quiet.

Then – a noise outside.

Pinbacker is in the Med Center.

INT. AIRLOCK – EMERGENCY LIGHTING

Capa hears Mace talking over the comms link.

MACE
(*over comms link*)
The mechanism is disabled. I can't lower the mainframe panels.

INT. ICARUS MAINFRAME – EMERGENCY LIGHTING

Mace is more talking to himself than Capa. He's working the console beside the tank, trying to lower the panels back into the coolant.

MACE
No, no . . .

The console is not responding.

The panels are clearly starting to short and malfunction.

They're going to burn out.

Mace yanks off his comms link –

– and jumps into the freezing coolant liquid.

INT. AIRLOCK – EMERGENCY LIGHTING

CAPA
(*shouting into comms link*)
Mace?

INT. ICARUS MAINFRAME – EMERGENCY LIGHTING

Mace's comms link sits by the side of the pool.

The liquid is only chest deep, but Mace is hyperventilating from the cold.

He pushes over to the first panel . . .

. . . working with numb fingers on the mechanism. Clumsy. Hands numb. But he manages to release a bolt manually, and the panel starts to slide down.

As the first panel slides into the coolant . . .

INT. CORRIDOR

In an empty corridor, the lights flicker on.

INT. AIRLOCK

Capa reacts to the sudden brightness.

INT. OXYGEN GARDEN

Light falls on Corazon's dead body . . .

. . . which, like Trey's body, appears to have been posed.

Her eyes are open.

Instead of lying, she is sitting like a Buddha.

In her lap, her hands rest, palms up.

And in her hands is the tiny green shoot.

INT. MED CENTER

Cassie jumps as the power returns, and the images return to the Earth Room walls – white clouds over blue sky.

Then, suddenly –

– the image on the opposite wall distorts and shatters.

And in its place, forcing through the smashed two-way –

– is Pinbacker.

The Earth Room malfunctions.

Multiple images of landscape flash as Pinbacker's face and bloody arm reach inside the smashed two-way.

The skin around his arm and hand has split from the action of smashing. The arm is slick with blood. Dripping and spraying.

Cassie pushes herself back against the far end of the room.

She's screaming.

Hyperventilating, failing to get the oxygen she needs.

Pinbacker starts to climb inside.

With the top half of his body through, he reaches out and grabs Cassie's arm . . .

She slashes at him with the scalpel.

His blood-slicked grip on her fails.

At that moment –

The Earth Room images suddenly flick to a busy city street. Thronging with people – as it might be Wall Street, at five minutes past one o'clock.

Pinbacker freezes – suddenly transfixed by the sight.

Cassie twists free, lunges at the door to the Earth Room, slips through, and runs.

INT. ICARUS II – FLICKERING LIGHT

Cassie runs through the spaceship, still holding the scalpel. Gasping. Sobbing.

Behind her, Pinbacker follows.

He passes through areas of pooled back-up/fibre-optic lighting, then areas of darkness, like a slow and strange strobe.

INT. ICARUS MAINFRAME – FLICKERING LIGHT

Mace has managed to haul himself out of the tank.

The cold is too severe for him to stay in the liquid. He kneels by the side of the tank, gasping, trembling, on his hands and knees.

He just about manages to compose himself. He reaches for the comms link. Lifts it to his mouth.

MACE

(*shaking uncontrollably*)

Capa – I don't know if I'm going to be able to do this.

CAPA

(*over comms link*)

Mace . . .

MACE

No time. Just listen. I'm going to try again. But if I fail, there's one last option.

He breaks off.

I know how you can get the ship out of orbit. (*Beat.*) Separate the payload.

INT. AIRLOCK – FLICKERING LIGHT

Capa holds the comms link.

MACE

(*repeats, over comms link*)

Separate the payload. Do you get it, Capa?

CAPA

. . . I get it.

MACE

Then you'll have to get to the bomb. And initiate it from the console. (*Beat.*) Don't ask me how. Just . . . (*Beat.*) Just make it happen.

A long beat.

MACE

(*over comms link*)

Okay. (*Beat.*) I'm going to do this.

CAPA

(*quiet*)

Copy, Mace.

MACE

(*over comms link*)

Copy.

And that was them saying goodbye.

INT. ICARUS MAINFRAME – FLICKERING LIGHT

Mace has slid back into the pool.

Hyperventilating again.

Movements slowing.

The second panel is sliding down.

He's working on the third.

Too cold now to speak.

His frozen hands can't work the third release bolt.

Fumbling. Failing.

His legs buckle.

He slips in. The coolant closes momentarily over his head.

Then he breaks the surface again, gasping, adrenaline and fear giving him strength.

His skin is splitting, cracking.

One last attempt with his claw hand at the mechanism . . .

. . . but he can't do it.

With the last of his strength, Mace pushes to the side of the tank . . .

INT. ICARUS II – FLICKERING LIGHT

The empty interior of the ship in flickering light.

INT. AIRLOCK – FLICKERING LIGHT

Capa stands, blood streaming through his fingers where he holds a hand to the wound on his stomach.

CAPA

. . . Mace?

Silence.

He lets the comms link drop.

EXT. ICARUS II

Icarus II orbits above the vast plains of fire below.

INT. AIRLOCK – FLICKERING LIGHT

We are on the reverse side of the glass from Capa, watching, in silence.

Capa is standing in one of the bulky space suits.

He has managed to put it all on –

– except the helmet.

Which, as has been established, can't be locked down by one man alone.

Capa puts the helmet over his head anyway.

We see him trying to reach his hands up to the locking mechanism – but it is impossible. The material of the suit won't allow such flexibility for him to reach up to the locking mechanism.

Capa stops a moment, propped up against the side of the airlock.

He is gathering strength . . .

Then he lowers his head like a bull about to charge . . .

. . . and hurls himself at the opposite airlock wall . . .

. . . head-butting the wall as hard as he can.

Even in silence, the impact looks horrible.

Capa falls to the floor.

Then picks himself up.

The tactic has worked. The helmet is attached.

Cut to Capa's side of the airlock.

Where Capa starts a series of actions we do not initially understand.

First, he takes the cutting tool from his utility belt that we saw him use with Kaneda, while fixing the shield panels.

Then he takes this tool, and uses it to cut a small hole in the glass of the inner airlock door.

Then he moves to the side of the airlock, and attaches himself to the wall.

And finally . . .

He reaches for the panel to the outer airlock door.

And pushes it.

A beat.

Then the door opens, into outer space.

A sudden rush of air as the airlock decompresses.

Then cut to the inner airlock door.

Where the ship's atmosphere is rushing out of the small hole.

And the glass around the hole is frosting. Then cracking.

And suddenly, the entire glass door gives way.

INT. ICARUS II – FLICKERING LIGHT

The ship decompresses.

Corazon's corpse is slammed through the narrow corridors, towards the depressurization point.

Ash, debris, objects – all fly through the ship, and eject from the open airlock.

But ultimately, the rush of air is faster than the loose objects within the ship.

INT. AIRLOCK – FLICKERING LIGHT

Once the ship has depressurized, Capa detaches himself from the airlock wall.

INT. ICARUS II – FLICKERING LIGHT

We follow Capa as he makes his way through the vacuum of the ship.

INT. FLIGHT DECK – FLICKERING LIGHT

Capa enters the Flight Deck.

He goes over to the pilot's console.

There he opens the protected switch which we saw Cassie use during the docking sequence between Icarus I and II, marked: PAYLOAD SEPARATION.

After lifting the protective panel . . .

He turns – towards the Icarus mainframe.

Behind the closed glass partition panel, he sees Mace.

In the same position as we last saw him. Slumped half out of the coolant tank.

Mace is gazing at Capa. He seems to be dead. Frozen.

Then he blinks.

Capa holds his gaze a few moments –

– then turns away.

He lifts his wrist, and sets a countdown on the digital timer.

Four minutes.

He starts the countdown.

Then taps in the password: SUNSHINE.

And turns the payload separation switch.

EXT. ICARUS II

The separation ring fires, and the payload section is propelled away from the rear section – just as we saw before.

INT. CORRIDOR INTERSECTION – FLICKERING LIGHT

Capa moves through Icarus II, heading now for the airlock between the front and rear sections of the ship.

En route, he encounters Trey's body, jammed unnaturally into a door frame. He has to move it to continue.

In the space suit, flickering light, and low gravity, movement through the ship is agonizingly slow and labored. It has the same quality as needing to run in a nightmare, but finding oneself locked into slow motion.

On Capa's countdown, this sequence takes approximately one and a half minutes . . .

INT. PAYLOAD AIRLOCK

. . . Meaning that as Capa reaches the airlock between the front and rear sections, he has only two minutes and thirty seconds left.

Capa opens the airlock . . .

. . . to reveal an amazing sight.

The Sun. Right in front of him.

And moving away from him fast, like a departing train, the payload section and shield.

Capa pushes himself into outer space . . .

. . . then fires his jet-pack.

EXT. SPACE

We watch as the tiny figure of Capa flies towards the payload bay.

Man has never seemed so alone or so exposed as in this image.

Behind him, as it falls out of the shield's protective shadow, the rear part of the Icarus II burns up.

INT. ICARUS MAINFRAME

Mace is in the coolant tank.

His face is frozen, motionless.

Then – he blinks.

Once. Still alive.

A moment later, he is consumed by fire.

EXT. PAYLOAD SECTION

Capa reaches the payload section.

For a few moments, he simply holds on to the outside of the vessel.

Behind him, as it falls out of the shield's protective shadow, the rear part of the Icarus II burns up.

Then Capa opens the airlock to the payload section, and enters.

INT. PAYLOAD AIRLOCK

The space suit lies on the floor.

Capa staggers away.

INT. OUTSIDE PAYLOAD BAY

Capa opens the hatch to the Payload Bay, entering onto one of the bomb's corners.

INT. PAYLOAD BAY

Capa stands on the surface of the bomb, looking at the huge flat expanse of silver before him. Ahead, in the middle of the space, is the ramp which leads down to the bomb's interior.

And, between Capa and the ramp, is Cassie.

She's sitting, head bowed, kneeling, in a pool of blood.

Capa takes a step towards her, and at that moment –

– there is a low, strange rumble. Distant thunder.

Capa looks at his watch.

The timer shows sixty seconds.

EXT. ICARUS II

Inside the vast halo of boosters that surrounds the payload section, a glow.

INT. PAYLOAD BAY

On Capa's face . . .

. . . as he feels the tremors of the boosters.

Then he crouches down, and we reveal he is by Cassie.

He gazes into her face, and sees –

– that she is badly wounded, but still alive.

Sticking out of her stomach is the scalpel blade.

CAPA

Cassie . . .

She just manages to raise her head to face him.

The boosters are powering up, the gravity is taking us. We're going to fly into the sun.

He takes her hand.

There's not much time.

Cassie is dying. She's distant, seeming only semi-aware of surroundings.

Capa tries to cut through her state of mind.

Cassie, I need to know. Where is he? Is he here?

And as he says this, dropping behind him in the one-sixth gravity –

– Pinbacker appears.

Over Capa's shoulder, Cassie sees as –

Pinbacker walks towards them.

Cassie's mouth moves – whispering something – but Capa can't hear.

Capa leans closer.

CASSIE
(*whispers*)

Behind you.

At that moment –

Reveal Pinbacker standing directly behind Capa.

Capa freezes. Sensing him . . .

. . . as on Capa's wrist, the countdown readout reaches zero.

And –

EXT. ICARUS II

– outside, the halo of boosters around the payload fires, in a colossal propulsive explosion.

INT. PAYLOAD BAY

On Pinbacker's face as he feels the power of the boosters.

PINBACKER

No . . .

Pinbacker's hand reaches down to Capa and violently rips him upwards.

Capa is thrown backwards –

– and lands strangely distant from Pinbacker.

He scrabbles back –

– Pinbacker is suddenly right beside him. Lifting him up by the neck.

Upright, to face each other.

Beat – as we stare in Pinbacker's eyes. Then –

PINBACKER

What's your name?

CAPA

. . . Capa.

Pinbacker throws Capa again –

– closer towards the edge of the bomb.

And with this throw, instead of following Capa, we stay with Pinbacker . . .

. . . who is distracted momentarily by a freakish sight.

Blood droplets are hanging in the air, spilled by Capa. They echo the movement as Capa was dragged upwards and thrown.

But instead of falling, they are remaining static, or poised, or orbiting each other, like miniature solar systems.

EXT. THE SUN

The ship flies down towards the Sun's surface.

INT. PAYLOAD BAY

Extreme close up on the faces of Capa and Pinbacker.

Their faces are vast. We can see the pores on their skin as craters, beads of sweat as biodomes.

PINBACKER

Capa – do you believe in God?

Beat – Capa's incomprehension that he is being asked this question.

Neither did I.

Pinbacker throws Capa again.

(*Calls.*) But I found him.

INT./EXT. PAYLOAD BAY/SUN

Cassie is still kneeling.

A blood droplet falls from a cut on her eye . . .

. . . rolling off her lashes, and dropping, with unnatural slowness, down to her lap.

As we orbit this droplet . . .

. . . it merges with the payload flying into the Sun . . .

PINBACKER
(*out of shot*)

In the sunshine.

. . . and Cassie looks up, and tilts her head, towards . . .

INT. PAYLOAD BAY

. . . Capa, at the edge of the bomb.

He looks behind him, into the void. Knows that next time he is thrown, it will be over the edge.

He rises, looking back at Pinbacker –

– who is running towards him.

EXT. ICARUS II

The payload contacts with the upper reaches of the Sun's surface, shattering the shield section into a thousand fragments of gold.

INT. PAYLOAD BAY

Pinbacker holds Capa by the neck. His feet are on the edge of the precipice.

PINBACKER

He told me to take us all to Heaven.

Pinbacker's hand squeezes tighter.

(*Gently.*) But Capa. We can't go to Heaven if you won't let us die.

INT. PAYLOAD BAY

Cassie, kneeling, pulls the knife out of her stomach.

INT. PAYLOAD BAY

In the earthquake violence of the payload's descent into the Sun's surface, and the roar of noise –

– Cassie appears, stepping out of the darkness behind Pinbacker.

Capa sees her.

Pinbacker senses her.

And half turns his head . . .

. . . as Cassie's arm reaches around him, with the knife in her hand –

– cutting across Pinbacker's upper arm, all the way to his neck, in one long deep slash.

Pinbacker lashes out, releasing Capa.

Cassie is struck, and sent over the edge of the bomb –

– and Pinbacker falls forwards.

But as he does so –

– he twists, and his hand snatches out, grabbing Capa.

For a moment they are poised, Pinbacker about to fall into the void, held only by his clutch of Capa's hand.

Then –

– around the top part of Pinbacker's arm, where it has been slashed by Cassie, a band appears, where the skin of his arm is separating from the skin of his shoulder.

The band expands – revealing the red slickness of exposed muscle beneath.

Then suddenly the entire skin of the arm sloughs away.

Pinbacker falls over the edge, into space.

INT. PAYLOAD BAY

In time distortion, Pinbacker and Cassie fall.

In the time distortions, behind Pinbacker, the blood streaming from his skinned arm hangs in the air like the trace from a firework.

He looks back at Capa as he falls – almost drifts – away from Capa, describing the same slow arc as the silver chess piece thrown between Capa and Searle.

INT. PAYLOAD BAY

Capa turns away from Pinbacker, and starts walking across the bomb towards the ramp.

EXT. THE SUN

And as the boosters and the gravity power the payload to impossible velocities –

– the endless movement of the Sun's boiling surface is slowing.

INT. STELLAR BOMB

In the bomb, a sliver of light appears.

Capa enters alone.

He stands on the gantry, surrounded by the sense of infinite darkness and space within the bomb.

At the far end of the gantry, the console.

INT. STELLAR BOMB

In the roof of the payload bay –

– in which fissures of amazing brightness are forming as the outer skin of the payload starts to burn away.

INT. STELLAR BOMB

Capa stands by the console.

His hands move across it.

The console is flickering and glowing, and number-crunch readouts are scrolling across the small monitor screen.

The scrolling data illuminates Capa's face.

Then suddenly, the data stops.

On the console, it reads: DETONATION INITIATED.

A beat.

Then Capa looks up.

Above him is a single dancing spark.

It fizzes and pops in the darkness.

Then splits in two.

EXT. ICARUS II

The outer skin of the payload is burned away.

INT. PAYLOAD BAY

Outside, on different surfaces of the bomb . . .

Pinbacker is falling.

Cassie is falling.

They are almost frozen.

A moment later, in a sudden rush, the fissures tear open –

– and the outer skin of the payload bay burns entirely away.

For a few time-distorted moments, we can see the silver bomb.

The Sun.

Cassie – seeing the Sun as if seeing God, and smiling.

Pinbacker – seeing God and screaming.

Then Cassie and Pinbacker are blown into vapor.

INT. STELLAR BOMB

Above Capa, the rapidly multiplying sparks fizz and pop, but remain in roughly the same location, moving like a fireflies.

He looks up.

Awed by the simplicity of the image, and the beauty . . .

. . . as the sparks multiply with exponential speed.

And fill the void.

Then suddenly –

The Sun breaks through the skin of the bomb.

A blazing fire, a flame wall, rushes down the gantry towards Capa.

And he is caught momentarily, between the Sun and the sparks.

And at that moment –

Time seems to almost stop.

The fire of the Sun is liquid before him, the dancing sparks become graceful.

And as Kaneda once did, Capa lifts his hand, towards the incandescence. As he does so, something falls from his grip.

Close up –

On Kaneda's chess piece, the silver king, falling slowly.

Cut to –

Star field

In a star field, caption:

8 MINUTES LATER

EXT. PARK – DAY

A park in the middle of a city.

A dog is being taken for a walk by a Woman.

We have seen the dog before, on a hologram photo: Maxwell.

By the light levels, we would estimate the time is either late afternoon or early morning.

The Woman throws a ball, and Maxwell runs after it . . .

. . . over the grass, to where the ball is bouncing.

He picks it up in his teeth . . .

. . . and as he does so, the light levels all seem to change . . .

. . . brightening.

No more dramatic than when the Sun appears from behind a cloud.

Maxwell looks up at the sky for a moment.

Then, with the ball still in his teeth, he starts running back towards the Woman.

End.

Sunshine

DRAWINGS AND STORYBOARDS

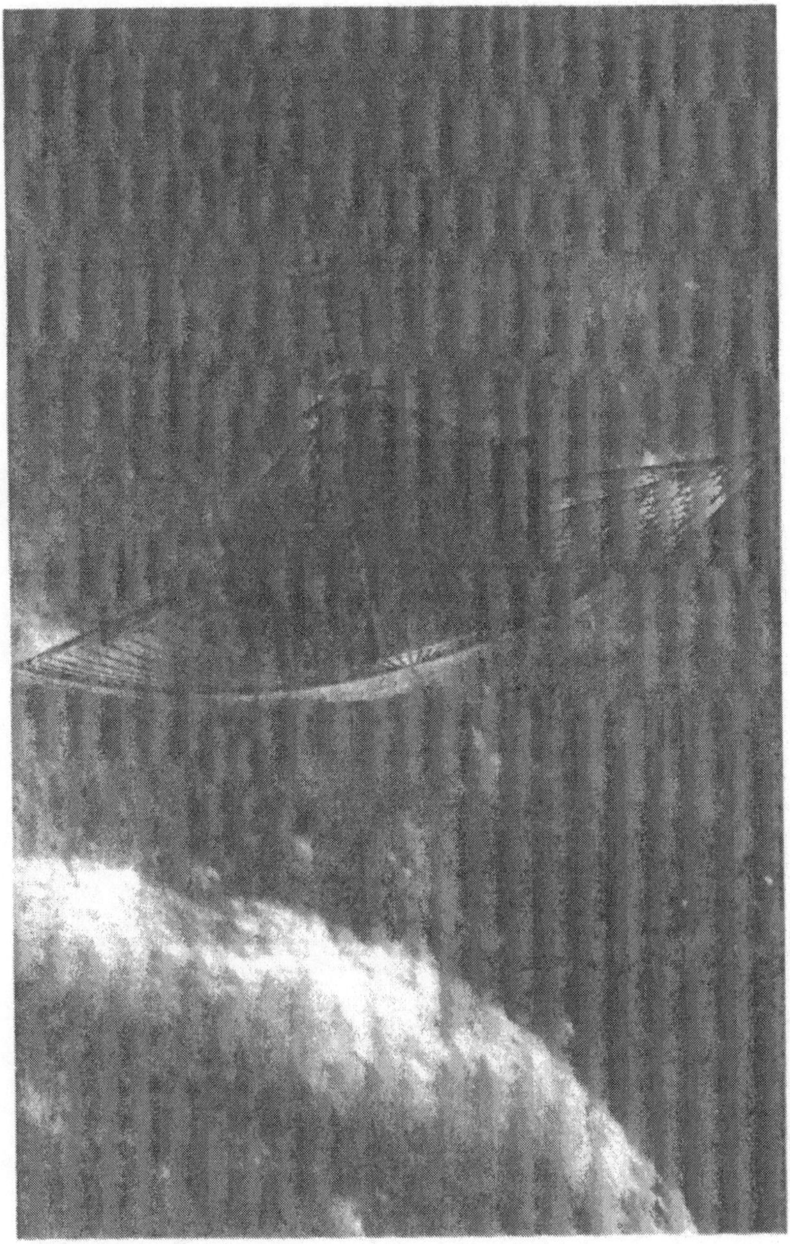

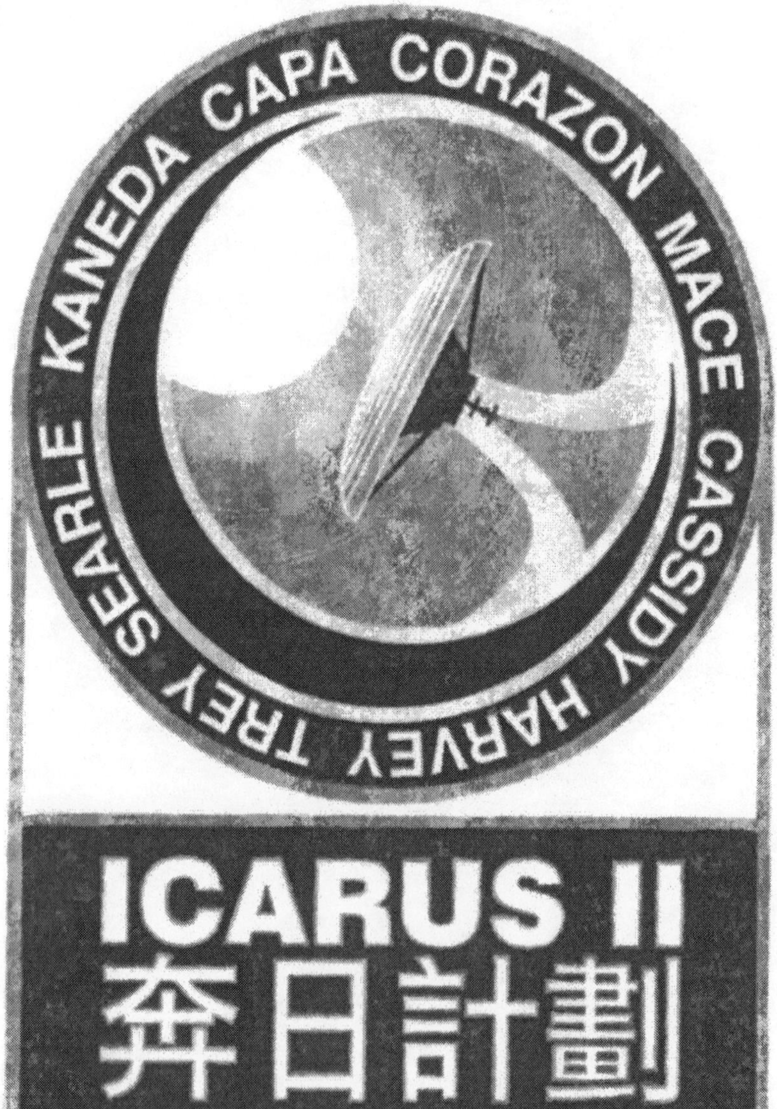
SEARLE KANEDA CAPA CORAZON MACE CASSIDY HARVEY TREY
ICARUS II
奔日計劃

CHOW
ROEG
WHITE
PINBACKER
FISCHER
NAKAZAWA
LIN
ESTEVES
ICARUS
奔日計劃

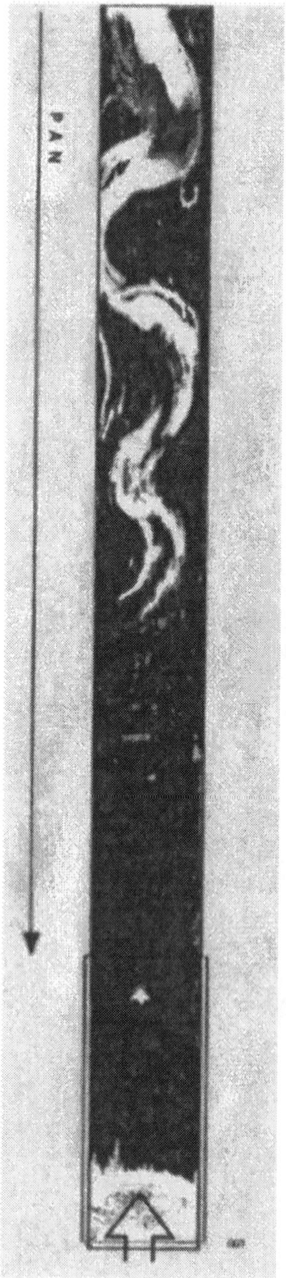

EXT. SOLAR FLARE

Icarus I floats in space . . .

. . . Icarus II comes into view.

Icarus I is the same design as Icarus II, but older, rougher.

In the sun-shaded section of the vast hull, the shield has been punctured in places through which indirect light reveals something of what is hidden behind the shields . . .

. . . a vast shape. Implied, but not revealed.

Icarus II comes alongside Icarus I.

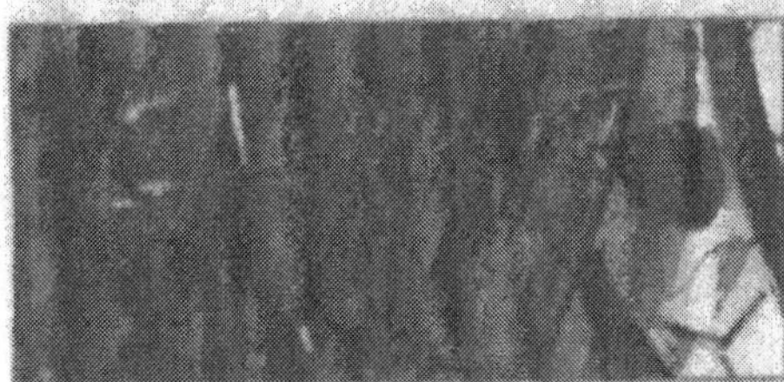

Icarus II moves in front of Icarus I.

FLIGHT DECK

Docking graphics.

Icarus II manouvers in front of Icarus I.

Then, continuing round the ship revealing . . . Icarus II, sunlit, closing in on Icarus I.

Jib up from Icarus I to Icarus II.

As the Oxygen Garden comes around, we see the inverted pyramid and, inside it, thick greenery.

And, between the greenery, what looks like an internal light.

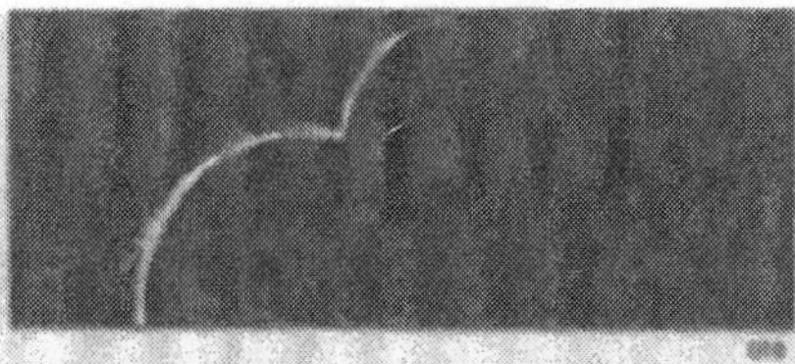

EXT. ICARUS II

The DOCKING SEQUENCE begins.

The two ships are positioned so that the shadows from their shields overlap.

The rear part of ICARUS II detaches from the main body of the ship.

This part, which contains all the living quarters, is the section that will perform the dock, within the overlap shadow caused by the two shields.

INT. AIRLOCK

CAPA, MACE, SEARLE and HARVEY stand in the airlock.

SEARLE is wearing his shades and he is very badly sunburned – his face a patchwork of red and peeling skin.

Silence. There is an oddly tense atmosphere.

Broken by Icarus: 'Airlock decompression complete. Ship-to-ship docking process will commence.'

Icarus II docking craft ignition.

Icarus II docking craft blasts away.

Icarus II docking craft reflected on surface of Icarus I.

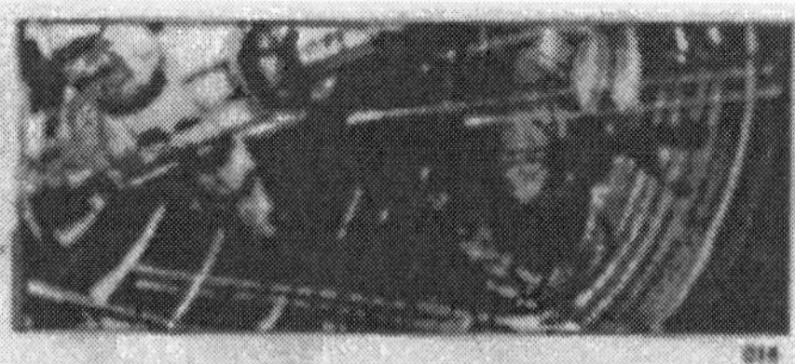

SEPARATE FLIGHT DECK SEQUENCE

MONITOR

MONITOR

MONITOR

MONITOR

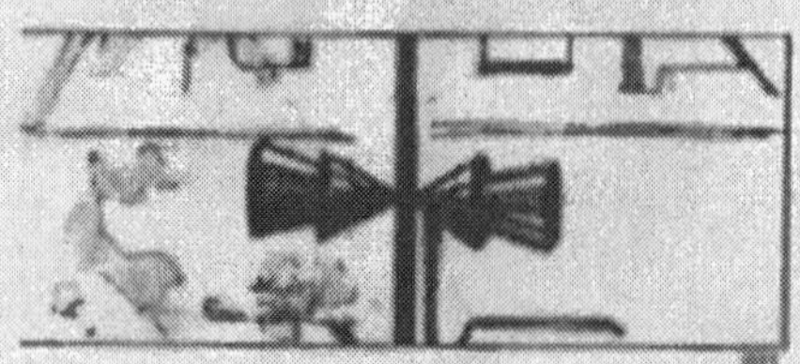

The two ships join.

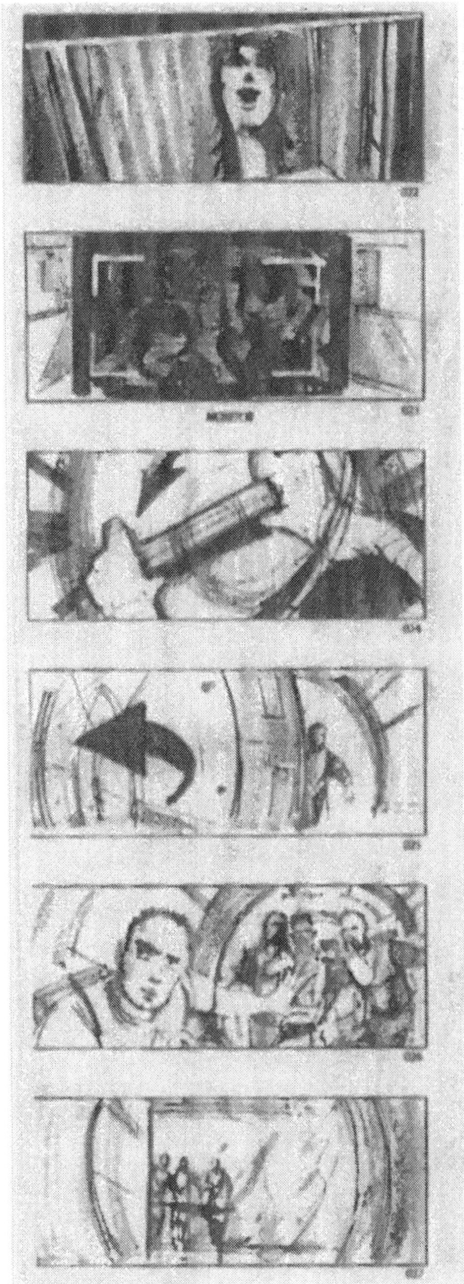

CASSIE. Okay. We're locked on. Icarus, please establish contact with Icarus I computer system.

ICARUS. Contact failed. Computer system of Icarus I has been disabled.

CASSIE. How? A malfunction or an accident? Has it been deliberately shut down?

ICARUS. Reasons unknown. Impossible to establish the cause remotely.

CASSIE. Is there power on Icarus I?

ICARUS. There is power on Icarus I. Solar harvest at full capacity, without detectable malfunction.

CORAZON. What's the atmosphere?

ICARUS. Oxygen-rich. Fully breathable and life-supporting.

CASSIE. Is it supporting any life?

ICARUS. Unknown. Impossible to establish remotely.

CASSIE. So you heard her. It's breathable in your own time, you're good to go. (*Beat.*) Be careful in there.

INT. ICARUS II AIRLOCK

Inside the Airlock of Icarus II.

The design of the interior of Icarus I is similar to Icarus II but feels slightly more dated, clearly an earlier model.

The airlock is dark, half-lit . . . until the airlock opens, revealing the bright interior of the Icarus II airlock, and the four men about to board.

Each carries a flashlight, and . . .

INT. FLIGHT DECK

. . . a head-cam, which are watched by CASSIE and CORAZON on the flight-deck monitor.

MACE. Doesn't look like there's a welcoming party.

INT ICARUS II AIRLOCK

The four sweep their flashlight beams around the dark airlock.

HARVEY. The air tastes . . . fine.

SEARLE. It tastes good.

Through window of Icarus I.

CAPA at speed up into shot.

CAPA turns to others.

BANG! As door opens, CAPA is dragged sideways through it.

CAPA. The mass of the plutonium in the payload is causing limited gravity.

HARVEY. We could try to get the centrifuge started.

Panic . . . They rush to the door.

CAPA. I wouldnt't. Everything will have rearranged towards the payload. Walls are going to be floors and floors will be walls. Starting the centrifuge again will be chaos. Let's just deal with what we've got.

MACE. Agreed.

CAPA laughs.

Immediately, all three men are sucked out into the airlock . . .

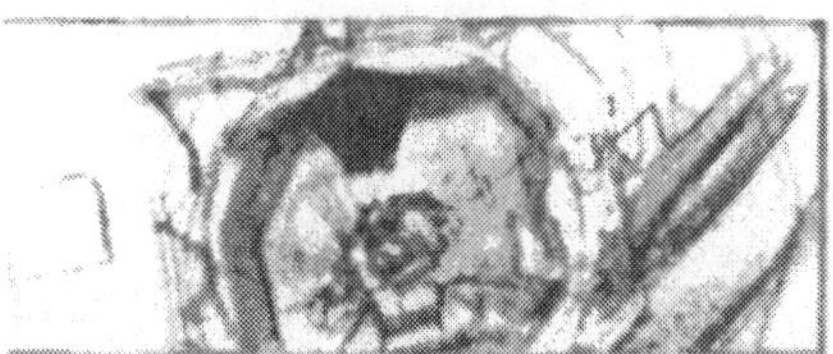

. . . then ejected though the broken outer door and into outer space.

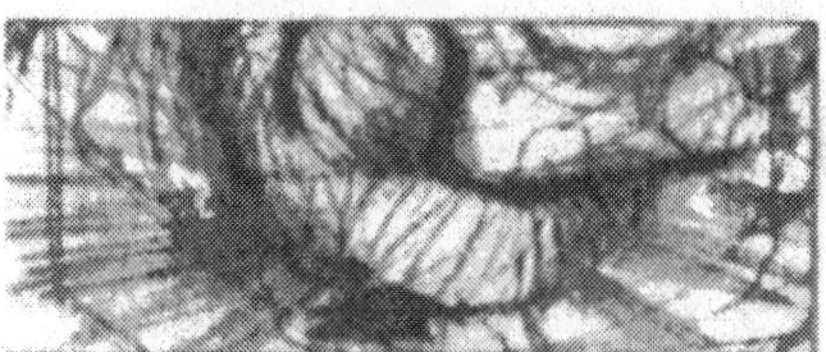

INT. ICARUS I AIRLOCK.

The three men shoot through the airlock, propelled by the evacuating gases.

As they pass through the broken area, HARVEY's shoulder catches twisted metal.

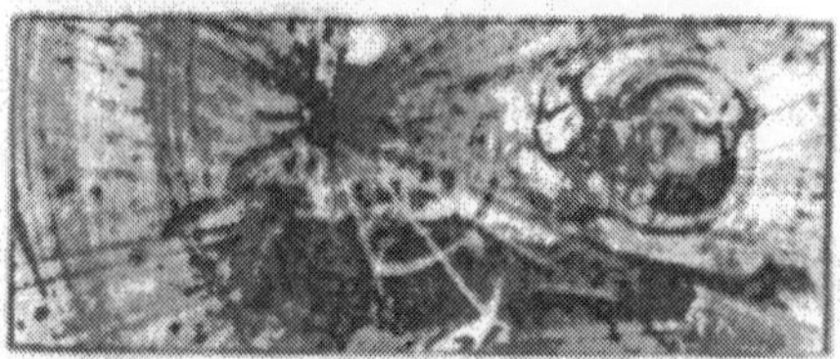

His shoulder visibly bleeds and he is wounded with a deep gash.

Blood sprays out – and freezes immediately.

EXT. ICARUS II

Silence as . . . we watch MACE, CAPA, and HARVEY shoot out from Icarus I towards Icarus II . . .

In the weightlessness of space, they have no control over themselves.

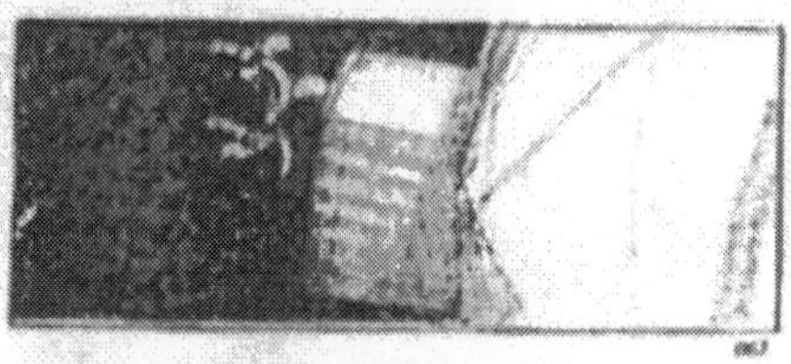

They fire across the short distance between Icarus I and II . . .

. . . then collide hard against the side of Icarus II.

The impact is shocking.

CAPA'a legs lock him into the airlock.

CASSIE operates the ship's cameras.

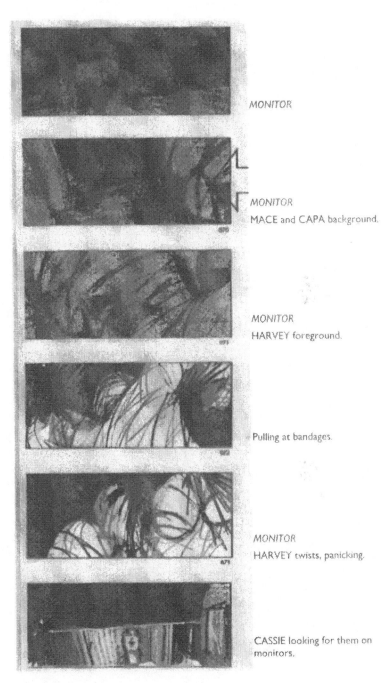

MONITOR

MONITOR

MACE and CAPA background.

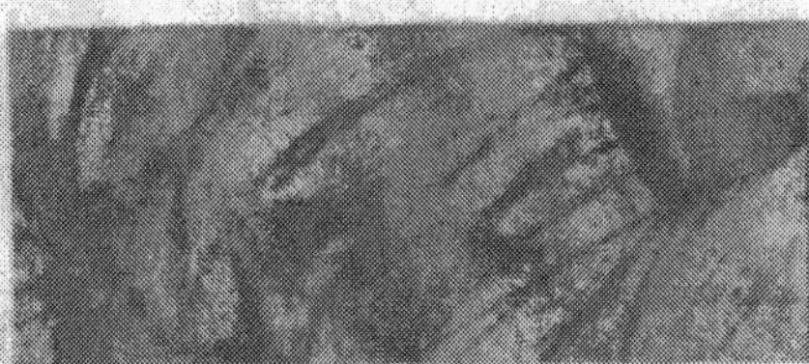

MONITOR

HARVEY foreground.

Pulling at bandages.

MONITOR

HARVEY twists, panicking.

CASSIE looking for them on monitors.

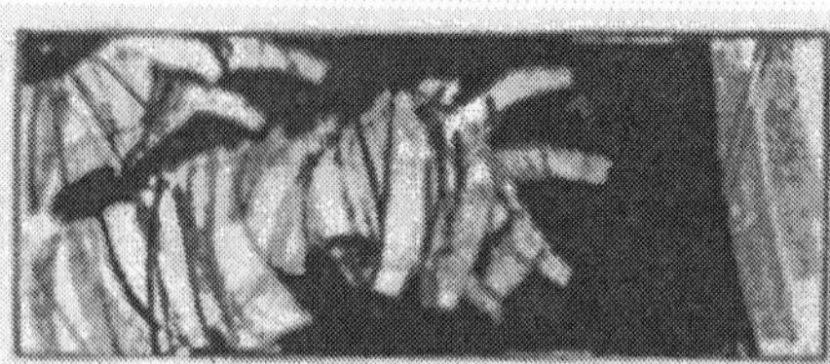

And now we can see that he is literally freezing as he falls.

His eyes open and ice over at once

CAPA clings on.

MACE bounces off, away from the airlock . . .

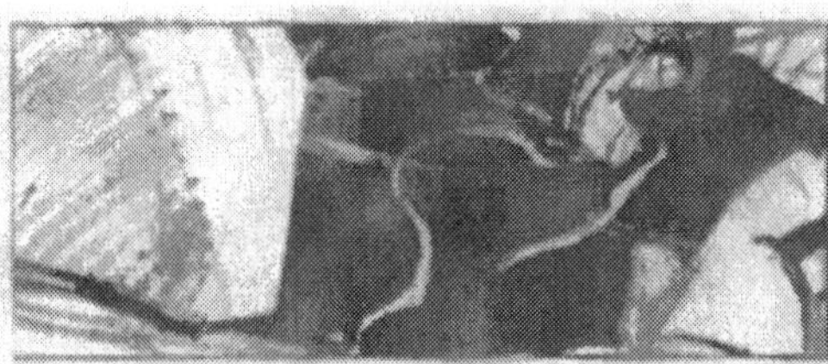

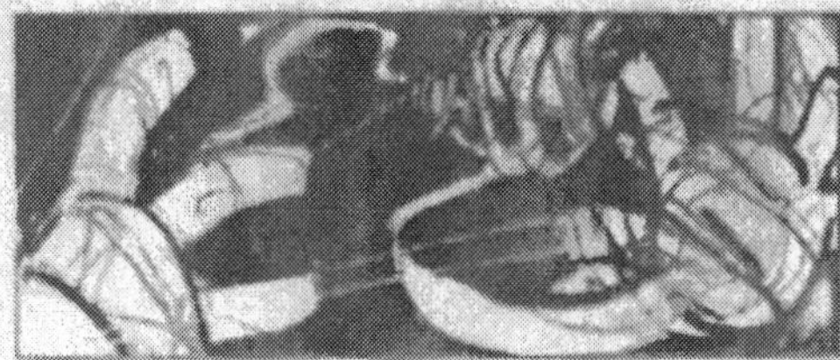

. . . But he is caught by CAPA.

MONITOR

HARVEY opens his mouth to scream . . .

. . . and as he does so, the moisture in his breath crystalises – hanging in a sparkling dust-cloud around his mouth.

In this posture, he dies.

But we stay with him.

Down the length of the ship, until his hand strikes a protuberance –

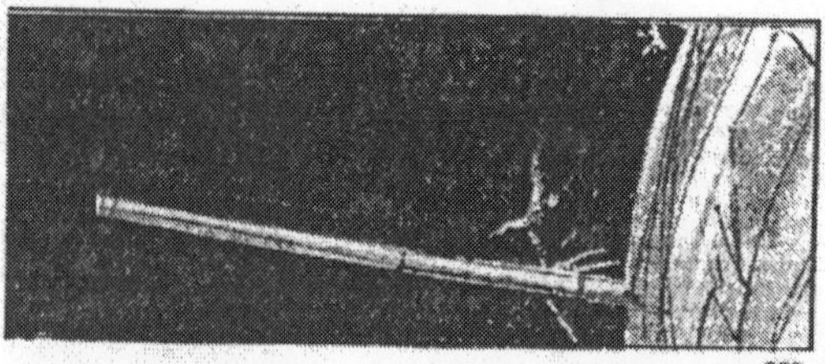

090

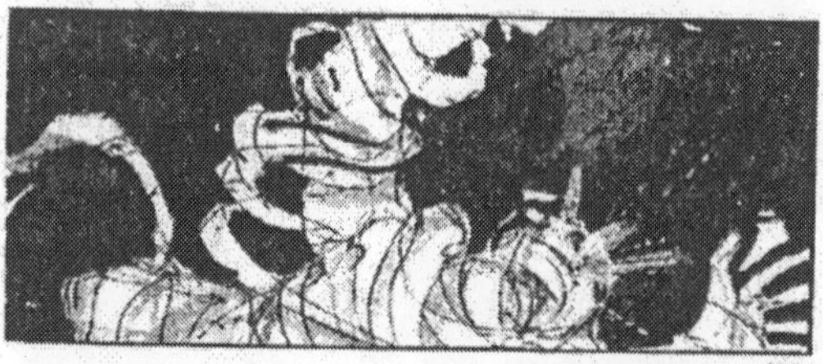

091

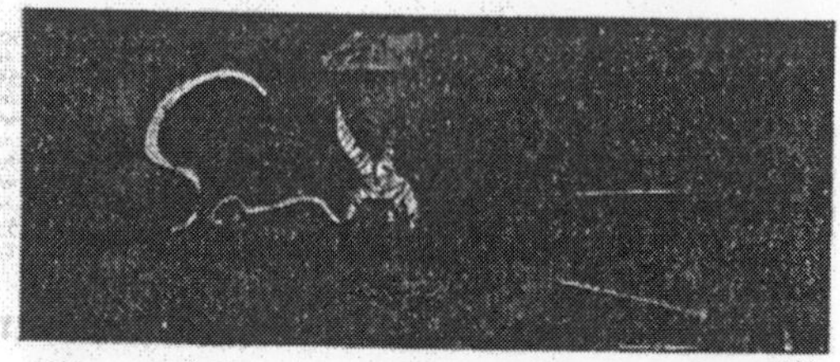

092

093

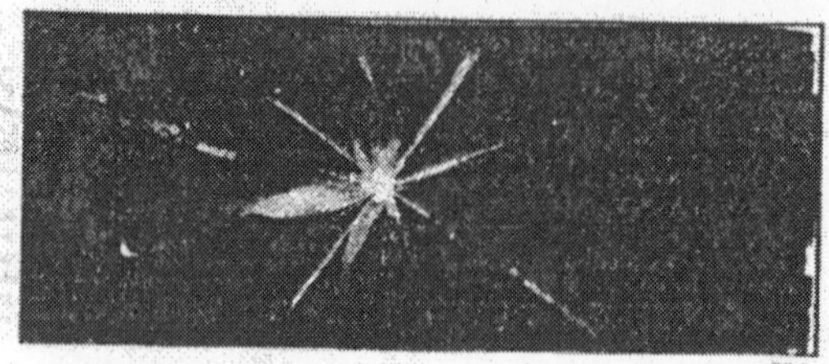

094

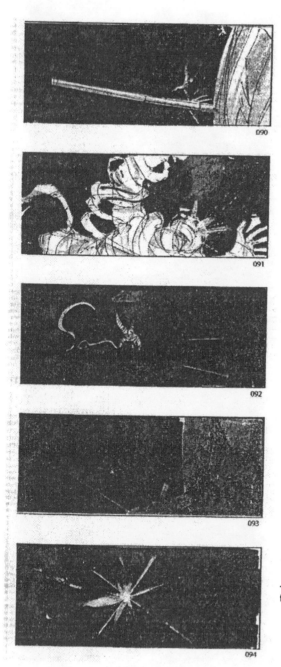

– until it is unshielded
from the sunlight.

35496037R00099

Made in the USA
Lexington, KY
13 September 2014